Whole School Character and Virtue Education

of related interest

Character Toolkit for Teachers
100+ Classroom and Whole School Character
Education Activities for 5- to 11-Year-Olds
Frederika Roberts and Elizabeth Wright
Foreword by Kristján Kristjánsson
ISBN 978 1 78592 490 3
eISBN 978 1 78450 879 1

Solutions Focused Special Education
Practical and Inclusive Strategies for All Educators
Edited by Nick Burnett
ISBN 978 1 78592 527 6
eISBN 978 1 78450 916 3

Teacher Education and Autism
A Research-Based Practical Handbook
Edited by Clare Lawrence
ISBN 978 1 78592 604 4
eISBN 978 1 78592 608 2

How to Be a Peaceful School
Practical Ideas, Stories and Inspiration
Edited by Anna Lubelska
ISBN 978 1 78592 156 8
eISBN 978 1 78450 424 3

Whole School Character and Virtue Education

A Pioneering Approach Helping all Children to Flourish

EDITED BY
PAULA NADINE ZWOZDIAK-MYERS

Jessica Kingsley Publishers
London and Philadelphia

Appendix B reproduced with permission of Department of Education.
Appendix C from Peterson, C. and Seligman, M. (2004) *Character Strengths and Virtues: A Handbook and Classification.* Washington, DC: American Psychological Association, pp.29–30. Reproduced with permission of the Licensor through PLSclear.

First published in 2020
by Jessica Kingsley Publishers
73 Collier Street
London N1 9BE, UK
and
400 Market Street, Suite 400
Philadelphia, PA 19106, USA

www.jkp.com

Copyright © Jessica Kingsley Publishers 2020

Front cover image source: Yeading Junior School

Library of Congress Cataloging in Publication Data
A CIP catalog record for this book is available from the Library of Congress

British Library Cataloguing in Publication Data
A CIP catalogue record for this book is available from the British Library

ISBN 978 1 78592 875 8
eISBN 978 1 78592 874 1

Printed and bound in Great Britain

Contents

Preface: Character Education in the 21st Century

PAULA NADINE ZWOZDIAK-MYERS

The inspiration for writing this book on character and virtue education at Yeading Junior School stems from two independent yet interrelated sources. The first concerns the call by the Department for Education (DfE) for evidence of ways in which schools can help to effectively shape and develop the character virtues of children that will ultimately lead to a better society. This builds on the vision put forward by Nicky Morgan (then Secretary of Education) in 2014, for England to become a 'global leader' in teaching character. Research by the DfE (2017) on developing character skills in schools, in collaboration with the National Centre for Social Research, sought to provide an evidence base for future policy and research, premised on the beliefs that desirable character traits 'can support academic attainment; are valued by employers; and, can enable children to make a positive contribution to British society' (DFE 2017, p.3). Although this research identified important factors schools felt were key to success, it did not wholly capture nor fully represent the quality or effectiveness of current provision and practice.

Therefore, the second source, in response to the first, concerns our principle aim to showcase how one unique case study primary school, situated within a pluralist community in the heart of West London, provides opportunities for children to develop *virtue literacy* and learn to become flourishing individuals within society. Rather than tracing this explicitly through the formal curriculum, other avenues have been purposefully selected to provide a more eclectic range of lenses through which this endeavour and transformative journey can be realized.

By way of introduction and to set the scene, what follows is an exploration of some meanings and understandings associated with character virtues, consideration of what can be understood by effective character education and its guiding principles, and analysis of some well-established (and emerging) frameworks of values and virtues that go beyond cultural and religious differences to express our common humanity and promote human flourishing within the 21st century.

Character virtues

Fashionable discourse in England concerning character virtues has seen a resurgent interest in Ancient Greek philosophy, especially that of Aristotle's notion of the flourishing pupil, in contradistinction to views that stem from various other Western ethical traditions, including such 18th-century Enlightenment thinkers as Kant and Hume. Since it is beyond the scope of this entry to review the philosophical history of character virtues, what is presented here is one version of virtue ethics amongst many possible others. This version captures Aristotelian perspectives of the concepts *aretê* (excellence, virtue), *phronêsis* (practical, moral wisdom) and *eudaimonia* (human flourishing, happiness) which give primacy to virtuous character.

From this tradition, a virtue can be understood as a character trait, which is a state of one's character. If a child possesses the virtues of courage, honesty and empathy, then courageous, honest and empathetic is the kind of child they are. That said, a child may appear to be a courageous, honest and empathetic person without actually being one, by ensuring she acts in certain ways. A child might, for example, choose to conceal what she knows to be a true account of a given situation from an authority figure so as not to betray a friend's confidence or fear of possible consequences that being honest may attract from peers. This means that to possess a virtue entails far more than a disposition to act in certain ways; amongst other things it requires that we act in certain ways for a certain type of reason.

In writing about virtues, Aristotle not only refers to character traits but also excellences of character. At the beginning of *Nicomachean Ethics* (*NE*) Book II, he distinguishes between two human excellences: those of thought and those of character. The latter (*êthikai aretai*), translated as 'moral virtue(s)' or 'moral excellences(s)', place emphasis on 'the combination of qualities that make an individual the sort of ethically admirable person he is'. Aristotle defines virtuous character as excellence (of character), a state concerned with choice, lying in a mean relative to us, determined by reason and the way in which the person of practical wisdom would determine it (*NE* II.16).

The mean Aristotle refers to here is not an arithmetic mean but one relative to the situation; and since each virtue is concerned with specific feelings or actions, it is no easy task – especially for children – to reach the mean. 'Anyone can get angry – that is easy – or give or spend money; but to do this to the right person, to the right extent, at the right time, with the right aim, and in the right way, that is not for everyone, nor is it easy.' Virtue is the state that makes a human being good and makes him perform his function well (*NE* 1106a15–24). His function (*ergo*) is rational activity, so when we exercise our fully developed rational powers well, when we realize our nature as rational beings, we are good (virtuous) human beings and live well (*NE* I.7).

In order to flourish and live well, a virtuous child's reasoning must incorporate correct conceptions of how to live, by recognizing that her own good is inextricably linked to the good of community (*NE* 1169a3–6). Social virtues of friendliness, generosity and mildness of temper, for example, are naturally formed through social bonds and relationships with others (*NE* IV.6–8). Through such friendships a child desires the good of another person, not for her own sake but for the sake of the other person; and within communities, such as our schools, economic and political arrangements are in place to promote conditions under which the conceptions of how to live well and develop social virtues enable children to become virtuous and to flourish.

Character virtues, once acquired, become strongly entrenched and 'go all the way down' (Hursthouse 1999, p.12) precisely because becoming virtuous is not simply a matter of being disposed to act in a certain way, but also to feel, respond and reason well.

Aristotle's concept of *phronêsis*, or practical wisdom, involves actions that reflect the morally correct virtue in the correct amount at a specific time and in a specific place. To apply this understanding to schooling, character educators must help children acquire the ability to see on each occasion, through nurturing, experience and habits, which course of action is best supported by reasoning. Practical wisdom cannot be acquired solely by children learning general rules; it also requires that they practise by engaging with those emotional, deliberative and social skills which enable them to situate their general understanding of character virtues into practice in ways appropriate to each occasion.

Aristotle also speaks of virtue as a unified, unconflicted state where emotional responses and rational assessments 'speak with the same voice' (*NE* 1102b28); in other words, the affective and cognitive elements of a child are in harmony, which indicates that the education of children's emotional responses is an important consideration for developing virtue literacy.

What becomes clear is that character virtues are complex multi-faceted phenomena, and, as Hudson (1986) remarks, 'the unity of character is extremely labyrinthine. It couples systematically a person's values, choices, desires, strength or weakness of will, emotions, feelings, perceptions, interests, expectations and sensibilities'. For those entrusted with cultivating virtuous children, the journey is both an exciting and a challenging one, with many windows of opportunity to explore for this important endeavour.

Character education

Underpinning any discussion of character education should be a clear vision of what the purpose of education is, what goals are worth striving for and what can be understood by a person of good character. From global, national and local contexts where character education is in evidence, responses to these fundamental questions of education and schooling may on the one hand look very different, whereas on the other hand, they reveal points of convergence. This section serves to illuminate some of these dis/connections as well as to demonstrate the significance of this field in cultivating virtuous children, as the following statement by Martin Luther King (1992, p.208) concerning the struggle for justice and democracy exemplifies: 'I have a dream my four little children will one day live in a nation where they will not be judged by the color of their skin but by the content of their character.'

In her book *The Death and Life of the Great American School System* several decades after King's famous 'I have a dream' speech, Diane Ravitch raised concern that the No Child Left Behind (NCLB) Act of 2001 created a national education policy that aimed to close the achievement gap through greater measures of accountability, flexibility and choice, yet neglected the central purpose of education 'to shape good human beings, good citizens, people of good character with the knowledge and skills to make their way in the world and to join with others to sustain and improve our democracy' (Ravitch 2010, p.245).

It was not until 2014 that character education truly reached Congress consciousness when the US Senate signed a resolution to introduce 'National Character Counts Week'. This declaration comprises 15 statements and signals that character education has become high status at the political level. These statements reveal a strong nationwide patriotic commitment from each and every citizen, community and organization, at a time when the country is fragmented on so many levels and at risk/under siege from internal and external social, political, global and economic forces. There is also commitment to democracy and an inclusive approach to US citizens and communities from diverse backgrounds.

Celebrating 'National Character Counts' for one week each year might seem to be an extraordinary notion, particularly since character building and developing virtuous children is, and has been, embedded within the everyday teaching and learning practices of educational contexts since schooling began. Which virtues dis/appear in the ethos, mission and vision statement of any school as well as their concomitant practices will be a reflection of the social, economic, geographical, political, ideological, religious and educational affiliations of time and place. For example, children's schooling experience of character building in England during Victorian times as compared to 21st-century learners, or children schooled within an Evangelical community in Mississippi as compared to a non-denominational community and school in New York City, will likely be quite different.

Notwithstanding the abovementioned resolution signed by Senate in 2014, character education in the USA has a long history, a very strong following and is big business! By the late 1800s at least two distinctive approaches to character education had emerged. The goal of the first was to teach traditional values and indoctrinate children with these. The second relativist approach was less concerned with teaching moral absolutes such as right and wrong; the goal was to focus more on teaching children to think critically about the reasons underpinning decisions they make when faced with moral/ethical dilemmas. Both approaches are prevalent in much contemporary schooling practice although, one could argue, they are more content specific in relation to moral lessons and the use of specific words and vocabulary.

Following a federal government-funded pilot project from 1995 to 2001, which 45 states signed up to (US Department of Education, 2008) the development of character education curricula became mandatory. The California Department of Education's response (Section 233.5a) in laying the groundwork for educators to *impress* upon children and young people the principles of character is as follows:

Each teacher shall endeavor to impress upon the minds of the pupils the principles of morality, truth, justice, patriotism, and a true comprehension of the rights, duties, and dignity of American citizenship, and the meaning of equality and human dignity, including the promotion of harmonious relations, kindness toward domestic pets and the humane treatment of living creatures, to teach them to avoid idleness, profanity, and falsehood, and to instruct them in manners and morals and the principles of a free government. Each teacher is also encouraged to create and foster an environment that encourages pupils to realize their full potential and that is free from discriminatory attitudes, practices, events, or activities, in order to prevent acts of hate violence. (California Department of Education 2019)

'Character Counts!', a programme based upon a framework developed by the Joseph and Edna Josephson Institute of Ethics, identifies '*Six Pillars of Character*'– Trustworthiness, Respect, Responsibility, Fairness, Caring, and Citizenship; and '*Four Wheels of Success*' – Academic Domain, Social and Emotional, Character, and School Climate. The eight goals underpinning the Character wheel of success are to:

- develop moral character and commitment in its use
- improve decision-making qualities
- demonstrate integrity, honesty, promise-keeping and loyalty, which are essential in relationship-building and career readiness
- demonstrate respect for authority figures and others without regard to gender, race, religion, sexual orientation or other distinguishing attributes
- make students accountable for their actions and the consequences of choices made
- increase cognitive skills related to being just and fair with others
- display compassion and a concern for the wellbeing of others
- demonstrate civic duties and social responsibilities.

The principle aim, behind Character Counts! through their programmes, workshops and resource materials, is to improve the ethical quality of society by advocating principled reasoning and ethical decision-making through a values-neutral (a somewhat contestable notion!) approach to moral education. Character Counts! has considerable influence nationwide, not only within schools but across a range of organizations, and emphasizes close cooperation between home and school. The six pillars, first proposed in the Aspen Declaration on Character Education (1992), were assumed to transcend cultural, religious and socioeconomic differences. Its working definition of character, influenced by Thomas

Lickona (1991), promotes the habits of thinking, feeling and doing. Schools are encouraged to foster these habits by developing statements that describe character expectations, provide a discipline policy to support goals, encourage participation in service projects and offer a range of extra curricula opportunities.

The view of children as moral agents is implicit within the expectations, rules and sanctions and kind of language used, as well as the lesson plans. Lawrence Kohlberg's (1981) work is drawn upon, albeit in an abridged way, to guide moral development:

> Elementary-age children are primarily concerned with their own survival – avoiding punishment and obtaining rewards by obeying the rules. Older children are motivated by the desire to gain approval from others (principally peers) and avoid disapproval. Only at the highest level of moral development are rules interpreted in terms of self-chosen principles. (Akin *et al.* 1995, p.2)

The programme is an ambitious enterprise and may be perceived as somewhat utopian, especially when the context of real life and lived experiences of children encountering pluralist competitive goods may be incongruent with the teaching and messages being conveyed.

The organization Character.org, with more than 20 years of experience, has a library of resources and tools to help create National and State Schools of Character, certified by their implementation of '11 Principles of Effective Character' (shown in Appendix A). In gaining recognition as 'Schools of Character':

> [A]dults embrace their critical role as models. Teachers work together as professionals – and with parents and community members as partners – to positively shape the social, emotional and character development of young people entrusted to them each day. Students in these schools feel safe, respected, connected to those around them, allowing them to thrive academically and socially and be motivated to give back to their communities. (Character.org n.d.)

In England, there has been much discussion in recent years about character education and the importance of embedding character education within our schools. A speech by the Secretary of Education, Damian Hinds, in 2019, categorized five foundations for building character: Sport, Creativity,

Performing, Volunteering and Membership, and the World of Work. Case study settings involved in the research commissioned by the DfE (2017, p.6) concerning the development of character skills in schools viewed their role as being to:

- encourage pupils to *understand, value* and *demonstrate* the positive behaviour traits that would make them well-rounded, grounded citizens
- support the development of the *skills* required to function in and contribute to society
- support social and emotional development, in order for pupils to better *understand themselves* and work on their weaknesses; and
- instil pupils with a *moral compass* and skills in understanding and interacting with other people.

It is important here to note that much policy discourse and writing in England concerning the development of character has historically been expressed in terms of a 'values-based' approach to education. For example, guidance documentation concerning the aims, goals and purposes of education, school curricula and the work of schools in England has resonance with that used in the USA under the term 'character education'. Appendix B reflects one such document produced by the DfE (2014, pp.5–6) for promoting fundamental British values as part of Social, Moral, Spiritual and Cultural (SMSC) education. Areas of congruence between both countries can be traced through aspects of character/values that contribute to personal development and individual liberty, mutual respect and equal opportunity for all, sustainable development and productive economy, and the rule of law, as well as a healthy and just democracy. Antecedents of guidance documentation related to character education in England can also be traced in such initiatives as Every Child Matters (ECM); personal, learning and thinking skills (PLTS); and, social and emotional aspects of learning (SEAL).

The Jubilee Centre for Character and Virtues at the University of Birmingham, founded in 2012 by Professor James Arthur, has established itself as a leading satellite centre for character education in England and has generated a wealth of resource material for academics, researchers and professional contexts. It defines character according to 'a neo-Aristotelian view of the psychology of moral development' (Jubilee Centre 2017, p.2): Flourishing individuals and society are underpinned by practical wisdom:

'the integrative virtue, developed through experience and critical reflection, which enables us to perceive, know, desire and act with good sense. This includes discerning, deliberative action in situations where virtues collide' (Jubilee Centre 2017, p.5). Character traits distinguished are: Intellectual Virtues, Moral Virtues, Civic Virtues and Performance Virtues. Virtue literacy as defined incorporates the components of Virtue: 'Perception', 'Knowledge and Understanding', and 'Reasoning' (Jubilee Centre 2017, p.8).

Key principles advanced by the Jubilee Centre for character education are presented in Appendix A alongside those of the '11 Principles of Effective Character' education from Character.org (n.d.) for comparative purposes. Schools in England that place character education central to their aims and vision, and meet criteria identified by the Centre, can be considered for, and recognized as, '*Schools of Character*' (Arthur and Harrison 2014). The country's first National School of Character was King's Leadership Academy Warrington, and the transformative journey of 'turning this school around' through the vision of 'Future Leaders and Education 2.0', underpinned by behavioural/psychological theories (e.g. human motivation, intelligence, mind-set and self-efficacy) has been well documented in a stimulating and thought-provoking way by the Associate Principal, a former officer in the Royal Air Force (Reay 2017).

The seven different kinds of case study school, including the aforementioned, featured within *Schools of Character* (Arthur and Harrison 2014, pp.35–6), showcase a variety of approaches to character education, yet reveal the following common strengths:

- vision and confident leadership
- critical mass of staff on board
- school as a community
- make character education visible
- caught and taught
- commitment to experiential learning
- time for personal reflection.

A more recent initiative of the Jubilee Centre is entitled '*Schools of Virtue*'. One key conviction upheld by the Centre is that virtues which make up good character can be learned and taught. To help primary and secondary schools evaluate their provision of character education, a guidance handbook has been produced with four sections: planning and evaluation; character caught – school ethos self-evaluation framework; character taught – perspectives on evaluating curriculum strategies and activities; and student self-reflection on character and virtues (Harrison, Arthur and Burn 2016).

The Centre for Real-World Learning, based at the University of Winchester, has been trying to address some fundamental moral questions concerning what we think 'young people need to know, believe, value and be able to do, if they are going to flourish in the complicated and turbulent world of the 21st century' (Claxton and Lucas 2013, p.5). Key to this pursuit, not dissimilar to that voiced earlier by Ravitch (2010), concerns the ever-changing focus and fashion of policy initiatives by successive governments – for example, high stakes testing, league tables, accountability measures and extremely 'narrow promotion of a particular set of moral beliefs and attitudes in the wake of the recent Trojan Horse Affair', which led to 'a drive to condition children in upholding fundamental British values' (Roach 2016). Since 2010, SEAL has been abandoned and curriculum space for personal, social and health education (PSHE) and sex and relationships education has been significantly reduced.

The Centre for Real-World Learning persuasively argues that those best placed to answer fundamental questions about the purpose/s of education and schooling are the school leaders themselves. Their synthesis of *qualities* and *virtues* that countries such as Australia, Ireland, New Zealand and Singapore singled out as desired outcomes of education and those of greatest value for 21st-century learners are as follows (implied antithesis in brackets):

Prosocial	**Epistemic**
Kind (not callous)	Inquisitive (not passive)
Generous (not greedy)	Resilient (not easily defeated)
Forgiving (not vindictive)	Imaginative (not literal)
Tolerant (not bigoted)	Craftsman-like (not slapdash)
Trustworthy (not deceitful)	Sceptical (not credulous)
Morally brave (not apathetic)	Collaborative (not selfish)
Convivial (not egotistical)	Thoughtful (not impulsive)
Ecological (not rapacious)	Practical (not only 'academic')

The prosocial desired outcomes of education are concerned with 'cultivating the attitudes of a good friend, a good neighbour or a good citizen' and the epistemic ones with 'qualities of mind of the powerful learner; a person who is able to meet difficulty and uncertainty with confidence, capability and enthusiasm' (Claxton and Lucas, 2013, p.9).

The Center for Curriculum Redesign (CCR) has also considered what children should learn for the 21st century at a time when 'humanity is facing severe difficulties at the societal, economic and personal levels' (Bialik *et al.* 2015, p.ii), which requires a concerted effort to cultivate personal growth and children's ability to fulfil 'social and community responsibilities as global citizens' (Bialik *et al.* 2015, p.1). The CCR proposes a holistic framework across four dimensions of education: *Character, Knowledge, Skills* and *Metacognition*. The broad aims of character (Bialik *et al.* 2015, p.1) are to:

- build a foundation for lifelong learning
- support successful relationships at home, in the community, and in the workplace
- develop the personal values and virtues for sustainable participation in a globalized world.

The CCR synthesized and refined many frameworks from around the world, incorporated concepts derived from theorists Edward Morin, Robert Sternberg and Howard Gardner, and contributions toward the final iteration of the Character framework were harnessed from more than 500 teachers across the globe. The six essential qualities of character that emerged from CCR's research are: *Mindfulness, Curiosity, Courage, Resilience, Ethics* and *Leadership*. This publication provides a detailed description of each quality along with their associated concepts and traits (with a caveat that these lists are by no means exhaustive), examples of how they can be learned and, as and where appropriate, possible methods of assessment.

Character strengths and virtues

We turn now to the field of positive psychology and classification of 'Character Strengths and Virtues' (CSV) by Peterson and Seligman (2004) from their analysis of eight moral and religious traditions (e.g. Ancient Greece and Confucius) that influence our understanding of socially valued patterns of behaviour. Framed around six overarching virtues claimed to be endorsed by almost every culture across the globe (*Wisdom and knowledge, Courage, Humanity, Justice, Temperance* and *Transcendence*), they identified particular strengths under each virtue, as shown in Appendix C, which met the following criteria (Seligman *et al.* 2005):

- ubiquity – widely recognized across cultures (as opposed to universality)
- fulfilling – contributes toward individual fulfilment, satisfaction and happiness broadly construed
- morally valued – in its own right and not as a means to an end
- does not diminish others – produces admiration and elevates those who witness it
- non-felicitous opposite – has obvious 'negative' antonyms
- trait-like – an individual difference with demonstrable stability and generality
- measurable – has successfully been measured by researchers as individual differences
- distinctiveness – not redundant with any other character strengths (conceptually or empirically)
- paragons – strikingly embodied in some individuals
- prodigies – precociously shown by some children or youth
- selective absence – missing altogether in some individuals
- institutions – deliberate target of social practices and rituals which try to cultivate it.

Further research led to the development of a character strength assessment tool known as the 'Values in Action Inventory of Strengths' (VIA-IS). Peterson (2006) proposed that character strengths lie along two dimensions: the x-axis reflects those directed toward the self (e.g. curiosity, learning) versus strengths focused on others (e.g. fairness, forgiveness); and the y-axis reflects those related to emotional expression – *strengths of the heart* (e.g. gratitude, zest) versus strengths related to intellectual restraint – *strengths of the mind* (e.g. learning, prudence). He argues that strengths close together may comfortably co-occur, whereas those further apart may be less compatible. This tool has been used to inform and analyze the impact of many positive education programmes and classroom interventions such as the Penn Resiliency Programme (PRP) and Strath Haven Positive Psychology Curriculum (Seligman *et al.* 2009).

The major goal of the PRP curriculum is to prevent anxiety and depression (the prevalence of which is worryingly high worldwide) by increasing children's capacity to handle day-to-day stressors and problems by teaching them to think more realistically and flexibly about problems they encounter. PRP also teaches assertiveness, coping strategies, decision-making and problem-solving skills. Key findings for the PRP as compared to control groups are that it:

- reduces and prevents symptoms of depression
- reduces hopelessness
- prevents clinical levels of depression and anxiety
- reduces and prevents anxiety
- may reduce behavioural problems
- works equally well for children of different racial/ethnic backgrounds.

In summary, research indicates that the PRP produces positive outcomes in children's mental health and wellbeing.

Major goals of the Positive Psychology Curriculum (PPC) are to help children identify their *signature character strengths* and increase their use in day-to-day life. The programme targets strengths (e.g. courage, kindness, wisdom) described in the VIA-IS classification valued across cultures. The intervention strives also to promote resilience, positive emotion and children's sense of meaning or purpose. Key findings for the PPC as compared to control groups are:

- increased engagement in learning, enjoyment of school and achievement (e.g. creativity, curiosity, love of learning)
- improved social skills (e.g. assertiveness, cooperation, empathy, self-control).

Schools across many parts of the globe have access to a wide array of such programmes and interventions to nurture character strengths and virtues, and tools such as the VIA-IS, are useful when trying to measure impact. Caution, however, needs to be exercised when attributing outcomes (even where control groups are used) for many reasons, not least the complex variables that comprise being human. Further considerations have to do with what constitutes evidence of change and how that change may be interpreted and by whom, particularly when self-reports and self-assessment serve as principle instruments. Similar concerns may be realized when questioning how schools make a judgement between 3 (very good implementation) and 4 (exemplary implementation) on items embedded within the character education quality standards (Character

Education Partnership 2008) aligned to 11 principles of effective character education (Character.org 2016).

Despite these reservations, the evidence base for effectively cultivating character strengths and virtues through a wide range of programmes and interventions, particularly in England, is gaining momentum. So much so, that research underpinning the 'character nation' Demos report with the Jubilee Centre for Character and Virtues (Birdwell, Scott and Reynolds 2015, pp.13–15) led to the following recommendations for government:

- create a statement of intent and a character framework for education providers
- assess character development: reform Ofsted
- embed character into school practices
- support and incentivize character education
- support teachers to develop character.

It is noteworthy (at the time of writing) that Damian Hinds announced plans to set up an advisory group to develop a 'set of benchmarks' for character education in England and to re-introduce the government's national character awards which had been 'shelved' in 2017 (Whittaker and Murray, 2019).

The treasure within

As a segue into the main body of this book, and returning to the fundamental question, 'What is the purpose of education?', the key recommendations embedded within the Delors report (UNESCO 1996) are no less significant today than they were over two decades ago. Tensions to be overcome, as recognized by the Commission (UNESCO 1996, pp.14–16) at that time, were between:

- the global and the local
- the universal and the individual
- tradition and modernity
- long-term and short-term considerations
- the need for competition and concern for equality of opportunity
- the extraordinary expansion of knowledge and human beings' capacity to assimilate it
- the spiritual and the material.

Four pillars of education underpin UNESCO's global vision of education both within and beyond schooling: *Learning to know, Learning to do, Learning to live together* and *Learning to be*. The pillars are inextricably linked, and the Commission placed greater emphasis on the pillar *Learning to live together* through two explicit strands – the discovery of others and experience of shared purposes:

> ...developing an understanding of others and their history, traditions and spiritual values and, on this basis, creating a new spirit which, guided by recognition of our growing interdependence and a common analysis of the risks and challenges of the future, would induce people to implement common projects or to manage inevitable conflicts in an intelligent and peaceful way. (UNESCO 1996, p.20)

The fourth pillar, *Learning to be*, combines the need for everyone in the 21st century to exercise 'greater independence and judgement with a stronger sense of personal responsibility for the attainment of common goals' (UNESCO 1996, p.21).

The notion of an integrated approach to education reflected in these four pillars has had significant influence on curriculum development, teacher training and policy frameworks in a range of countries worldwide. For example, the report entitled *Learning to Live Together: Education Policies and Realities in the Asia-Pacific* (UNESCO 2014) maps out how this vision has been translated into the education systems of Afghanistan, Australia, Indonesia, Malaysia, Myanmar, Nepal, Philippines, Republic of Korea, Sri Lanka and Thailand.

What this and similar reports undertaken by UNESCO reveal is that the four pillars of learning may be under threat and in need of reinterpretation, especially when viewed through the lens of current worldwide and societal challenges. Those of *Learning to be* and *Learning to live together*, in particular, need to reflect such concerns as global citizenship, poverty, child exploitation and slavery, displaced orphans and refugees, quality education for all, conflict in war zones, natural disasters and sustainable development. In *Rethinking Education: Towards a Global Common Good?*, UNESCO calls for a strengthening of ethical principles and humanistic values which are to incorporate 'respect for life and human dignity, equal rights and social justice, cultural and social diversity; and a sense of human solidarity and shared responsibility for our common future' (2015, p.38).

These aspirations bring us full circle to Aristotle's translation of *phronêsis,* or practical wisdom, which incorporates those actions which reflect the morally correct virtue in the correct amount at a specific time and in a specific place. In their endeavour to cultivate virtuous children for the 21st century, in all its complexity and richness, Yeading Junior School embraces each of the four pillars of learning in multifarious ways both to unlock and celebrate that, which is *the treasure within*.

Chapters within this book have been written by professional practitioners, each of whom has a wealth of experience and expertise from a diverse range of educational settings. These contributions serve to reflect their own bodies of work, frames of reference, ideologies, perspectives and commitments to the promotion of character and virtue education at Yeading Junior School. Chapter 1 contextualizes the school's history and background and illustrates how policy change as well as global initiatives over time have influenced decisions taken to situate character education across life, both at the school and beyond. Chapter 2 demonstrates how a strong interfaith ethos can enhance character education and develop the virtues of children and young people. The story of language learning and acquisition featured within Chapter 3 is set not only against the national policy landscape and introduction of compulsory language teaching in primary schools across England from 2014, but also against the emergence of Latin through engagement with the wholly inclusive 'Classics for All' project. Chapter 4 explains the goals and purposes behind the multifarious web of networks and partnerships embedded within and embraced by Yeading Junior School, which incorporates ways in which a set of virtues can be nurtured through social action and involvement with Team London and the WE Schools movement.[1] Intergenerational learning is the focus of Chapter 5, which describes how a programme of interventions can support children's development of character and virtue education alongside stimulating social contact and communication between

---

1   WE Schools promote an innovative series of experiential social action programmes that engage teachers and young people globally to empower them with the skills, knowledge and motivation to bring positive change in themselves and the world. WE is an organization that brings people together and gives them the tools to change the world. A unique family of organizations, WE is made up of WE Charity, empowering change with resources that create sustainable impact, and ME to WE, a social enterprise that creates socially conscious products and experiences that allow people to do good through their everyday choices. The celebration of that change happens at WE Day – inspiring stadium-sized life-changing events that take place around the world. A movement of 3.4 million young people supporting 2,500+ local and global causes, we've provided more than 1 million people with clean water and built 1,000 schools and school rooms overseas, giving more than 200,000 children access to education. WE was founded more than 20 years ago by humanitarians, activists and social entrepreneurs, brothers Craig and Marc Kielburger. For more information visit www.we.org

multiple generations to improve the emotional health and wellbeing of all those involved. Chapter 6 discusses ways in which the Children and Families team at Yeading Junior School facilitate a nurturing environment within the Me Zone by offering a range of strategies and support groups underpinned by character and virtue education, such as the Marlborough Project which is an eight-week programme designed to look at the 'whole of the child' including their family and home environment. Recognized as a centre of excellence in financial education with Young Enterprise, Chapter 7 describes the introduction and progression of financial literacy within the school and exemplifies how character virtues are practised on a day-to-day basis and encompass the essence of citizenship. Chapter 8 is concerned with engendering pride and the road to achievement through an exploration of individual aspects of school, where success has led to further success: it is one of celebration, commitments and lessons learned, informed by the character virtues embedded within the ethos of the school.

The concluding section, Endnote, reflects upon ways in which character and virtue education has been interpreted and is practised within and beyond the school gates of Yeading Junior School at the time of writing, and considers future possibilities and directions of travel in relation to the cultivation of virtuous children.

References

Akin, T., Dunne, G., Palomares, S. and Schilling, D. (1995) *Character Education in America's Schools.* Torrance, CA: Inner Choice Publishing Company.

Aristotle (1984) *Nicomachean Ethics* and *Politics.* In J. Barnes (ed.) *The Complete Works of Aristotle* (2 vols). Princeton, NJ: Princeton University Press.

Arthur, J. and Harrison, T. (2014) *Schools of Character.* Birmingham: The Jubilee Centre for Character and Virtues (University of Birmingham).

Aspen Declaration on Character Education (1992) Accessed 12/05/19 at www.charactercounts. org/program-overview

Bialik, M., Bogan, M., Fadel, C. and Horvathova, M. (2015) *Character Education for the 21st Century: What Should Students Learn?* Boston, MA: Center for Curriculum Redesign. Accessed 27/03/19 at www.curriculumredesign.org

Birdwell, J., Scott, R. and Reynolds, L. (2015) *Character Nation: A Demos Report with the Jubilee Centre for Character and Virtues.* Accessed 25/04/10 at www.demos.co.uk/files/476_1505_ characternation_web.pdf?1433340847

California Department of Education (2019) *The Role of Character Education in Public Schools.* Accessed 15/05/19 at www.cde.ca.gov (search for character education)

Character Counts! (n.d.) Program overview. Accessed 12/05/10 at https://charactercounts.org/ program-overview

Character Education Partnership (2008) *Character Education Quality Standards.* Accessed 27/03/19 at www.character.org/?s=Character+Education+Quality+Standards

Character.org (n.d.) 'The 11 Principles of Effective Character.' Accessed 10/04/19 at www. character.org/character

Claxton, G. and Lucas, B. (2013) *Redesigning Schooling-2: What Kind of Teaching for What Kind of Learning?* London: The Schools Network (SSAT) Ltd.

Department for Education (DFE) (2014)*Promoting Fundamental British Values as Part of SMSC in Schools.* Departmental advice for maintained schools. DfE-00679-2014. Accessed 18/04/19 at www.gov.uk/government/publications/promoting-fundamental-british-values-through-smsc

Department for Education (DFE) (2017) *Developing Character Skills in Schools.* DFE-RR697a. National Centre for Social Research. Accessed 20/03/19 at www.gov.uk/government/publications/developing-character-skills-in-schools

Harrison, T., Arthur, J. and Burn, E. (2016) *Character Education: Evaluation Handbook for Schools.* Birmingham: The Jubilee Centre for Character and Virtues (University of Birmingham).

Hinds, D. (2019) 'Education Secretary sets out five foundations to build character.' Speech at the Church of England Foundation for Educational Leadership conference, 7 February. Accessed 20/05/19 at www.gov.uk/government/speeches/education-secretary-sets-out-five-foundations-to-build-character

Hudson, S. (1986) *Human Character and Morality: Reflections from the History of Ideas.* Boston, MA: Routledge & Kegan Paul.

Hursthouse, R. (1999) *On Virtue Ethics.* Oxford: Oxford University Press.

Jubilee Centre for Character and Virtues (2017) *A Framework for Character Education in Schools.* Birmingham: University of Birmingham. Accessed 08/27/18 at www.jubileecentre.ac.uk

King, M. L. (1992) 'I have a dream.' In C. Ricks and W. Vance (eds) *The Faber Book of America.* London: Faber and Faber.

Kohlberg, L. (1981) *The Philosophy of Moral Development Volume 1: Essays on Moral Development.* San Francisco, CA: Harper Collins

Lickona, T. (1991) *Educating for Character.* New York, NY: Bantam Books.

Peterson, C. (2006) *A Primer in Positive Psychology.* Oxford: Oxford University Press.

Peterson, C. and Seligman, M. (2004) *Character Strengths and Virtues: A Handbook and Classification.* Washington, DC: American Psychological Association.

Ravitch, D. (2010) *The Death and Life of the Great American School System: How Testing and Choice Are Undermining Education.* New York, NY: Basic Books.

Reay, A. (2017) *The Power of Character: Lessons from the Frontline.* Woodbridge: John Catt Educational Limited.

Roach, P. (2016) 'Teaching Character: The contribution of teachers to character education.' *Character, Values and Ethics: Research Intelligence 130,* 22–23.

Seligman, M., Ernst, R., Gillham, J., Reivich, K. and Linkins, M. (2009) 'Positive education: Positive psychology and classroom interventions.' *Oxford Review of Education 35*(3), 293–311.

Seligman, M., Steen, T., Park, N. and Peterson, C. (2005) 'Positive psychology progress: Empirical validation of interventions.' *American Psychologist 60*(5), 410–421.

United Nations Educational, Scientific and Cultural Organization (UNESCO) (1996) *Learning: The Treasure Within.* The Delors Report. Paris: UNESCO.

United Nations Educational, Scientific and Cultural Organization (UNESCO) (2014) *Learning to Live Together: Education Policies and Realities in the Asia-Pacific.* Paris: UNESCO.

United Nations Educational, Scientific and Cultural Organization (UNESCO) (2015) *Rethinking Education: Towards a Global Common Good?* Paris: UNESCO.

United States Department of Education (2008) *Partnerships in Education Program: State Pilot Projects 1995–2001, Lessons Learned.* Accessed 12/05/19 at www2.ed.gov/charactered/lessons.pdf

Chapter 1

Why Character Education at Yeading Junior School?

CAROLE JONES

Yeading Junior School is a richly diverse community of learners where ambition flourishes and commitment to learning is a real strength. Housed in its 1932 brick building, this four-form entry junior school (Years 3, 4, 5 and 6) extends its reach, both locally and nationally, in its endeavours to offer children the best possible opportunities to grow in life. Building networks, links and relationships is at the heart of the school's drive to create an exciting, dynamic environment where learners are not only successful but have the ability to make a difference to themselves and the world around them. As Daniel Goleman writes:

> If your emotional abilities aren't in hand, if you don't have self-awareness, if you are not able to manage your distressing emotions, if you can't have empathy and have effective relationships, then no matter how smart you are, you are not going to get very far. (Goleman 1998, p.317)

Education is about so much more than academic achievement at Yeading Junior School. It is about the development of the whole child, enabling each individual to take their place in society with confidence, ambition and determination and a strong moral understanding.

This chapter charts the ways in which this large junior school has undergone a deepening journey into developing the social, emotional and moral aspects of learners in a creative way across the curriculum. Character education is central to the work of Yeading Junior School, and, in the words of Mahatma Ghandi, 'We but mirror the world. All the tendencies present in the outer world are to be found in the world of our body. If we could change ourselves, the tendencies of the world would also change' (cited in Dhiman 2015, p.101). This message is cultivated with our children in all aspects of the life and work of the school.

The thrust for this work has been born out of a strong desire to ensure that our bright and enthusiastic young children should also be confident and articulate in all situations as well as enabling them to understand how our actions impact on others. Many learners (approximately 84 per cent) speak more than one language and over 30 per cent are entitled to Pupil Premium.[1] The school is situated in a known area of deprivation, but the intake remains fairly mixed, with a considerable element of mobility. Parental engagement is strong as indeed are the parents' aspirations for their children. Over time, Pupil Voice has become a strong element. The school's interface with others, including local, global organizations and community groups, has been recognized and valued.

Initially, much of the school's work linked with emotional wellbeing – setting up peer supporters and anti-bullying ambassadors and instilling an understanding of the impact of social action on others as well as oneself. One example of this has been cited in a short case study, featuring a former pupil, from the Council on Social Action (CoSA) (2008) entitled 'Side by side: A report setting out the Council on Social Action's work on one-to-one'. The school has first-hand knowledge that this pupil continued to excel at secondary school, secured an excellent university place reading Medicine having achieved high examination grades, and is continuing to undertake social action.

The school has undertaken much work within the local community through such ventures as litter picks, working with other schools to form a community choir, establishing its own currency, and, teaching learners about 'wants and needs' and the impact of loan sharks on families (Codd 2014). An interfaith network has been established and greater understanding of our commonalities has been shared through faith groups and acquiring knowledge of different cultures. Particular activities have included hosting special inspirational visitors, and working with charities and other organizations. The school features as a small case study in the #iwill campaign[2] and has completely embraced the work of WE Schools

---

1   The Pupil Premium grant is awarded to schools for the purpose of supporting disadvantaged children (e.g. based upon children's eligibility for Free School Meals according to a set of criteria).

2   The #iwill campaign is a UK-wide initiative that promotes practical action in the service of others (its aims are more fully explained in Chapter 8). For further details, please visit www.iwill.org.uk

(see Preface). This global movement was brought to Yeading Junior School by an inspirational speaker from Team London and has, especially in more recent years, become a major sphere of influence. Small groups of children have engaged in our intergenerational work, guiding and supporting older members of the Northwood Live at Home Scheme with iPad training and entertaining them through drama, song and dance (as detailed in Chapter 5). City Pitch, another Team London activity, has enabled us to gain funds to support the local community, thus enabling the children to demonstrate the qualities and virtues to which we as a school aspire. Collectively, such programmes as these, and the opportunities they afford, contribute towards our good behaviour policy and enable children to role model good character traits, which lead to improved attainment and an improved commitment to learning.

Character education is central to the life of our school, aligning to both its ethos and vision. It is essentially a whole school approach to building character, involving all things and all people. The school has set up leads amongst staff – both teaching and non-teaching members – and also, significantly, children leads. A mentoring approach has been developed and, initially, at the embryonic stage, we selected 12 Year 6 children to be inducted into the role of special 'Agents of Change'. This model proved to be most effective and had the desired result of effecting change amongst others. Taking this forward, we now currently have 26 active and thriving 'Agents of Change' who lead on a range of projects and activities. They are strong role models for others to emulate and are selected on an annual basis through application and rigorous interview, as their influence is so great. The letters of application for this role are extremely well written and show a great understanding of what is required. A majority of the children have been able to cite evidence of the multiple ways in which they have already made changes in their school or wider community. These children have been particularly instrumental in supporting others to inculcate the following ten character virtues which are embedded within the ethos of our school, across all projects and activities:

Resilience – Respect – Dignity – Teamwork – Compassion – Volunteering – Determination – Reflection – Pride – Curiosity

The school works very closely with organizations such as the previously mentioned Team London and #iwill. We consider that all children and staff within our school have the capacity to be 'Agents of Change' and work through the character virtues to achieve this. Through social action we not only achieve change within our school but also support local causes and global issues. To evaluate the impact of our initiatives and activities, we have gathered and used empirical evidence; for example, observing attitudes throughout the school in relation to academic work, creative learning and sport. There is a very notable and visible change in terms of interaction, self-discipline, determination, curiosity, positive attitudes and pride. In an article entitled 'Why there's no such thing as a gifted child', Wendy Berliner states:

> According to my colleague, Prof Deborah Eyre, with whom I've collaborated on the book *Great Minds and How to Grow Them*, the latest neuroscience and psychological research suggests most people, unless they are cognitively impaired, can reach standards of performance associated in school with the gifted and talented. However, they must be taught the right attitudes and approaches to their learning and develop the attributes of high performers – curiosity, persistence and hard work, for example – an approach Eyre calls 'high performance learning'. Critically, they need the right support in developing those approaches at home as well as at school. (Berliner 2017)

This particular article was drawn to my attention by a visitor who had observed an assembly about one of the virtues we use at our school: Curiosity. The visitor was truly impressed by the quality of the children's presentation and depth of knowledge and understanding portrayed, attributing this to the school's work on character and also linking it to pupil's progress. Recent letters written by children indicate how they reflect on their learning and attitudes and acknowledge personal changes that could improve their learning or future. The example below exemplifies a piece of written work about curiosity which was produced by a child in Year 6.

Curiosity is being curious and asking questions.
    In our everyday lives, we always use curiosity. When we are learning, we always try to ask as many extraordinary questions as we can. Many things around us such as the bright light bulb invention, used curiosity in its making. Here are some of the places we use this amazing virtue:

- when learning a new topic
- discover a new subject, word or topic

- how things around us operate
- what others' jobs are about
- learning more about an object or living thing.

Curiosity is an incredible thing to have, as it has many advantages, like boosting your knowledge. It can help give an interest in something.

Children clearly demonstrate positive attitudes in class reflecting wholeheartedly on the virtues; likewise through assemblies and through external projects and networks with others. They are very keen to show these changes and share the virtues with their families. Each class assembly with invited parents has a virtue theme threaded throughout it, which serves to reinforce the importance of harnessing these character virtues in all aspects of the children's learning and lives. We use the character virtues as transferrable skills to improve learning. We seize every opportunity for the children to reflect upon these skills and demonstrate their understanding of these virtues in wider arenas.

Volunteering and social action

The notion of selflessly helping others has been present in our school for a number of years. Children willingly take on volunteer roles throughout the school; for example, each class has a bank manager for our Bank of Yeading, and each class has two representatives on the Voice Box (our pupil voice), as well as playground buddies, Eco supporters and much more from classes across the school. The children also entered a choir competition, a first for the school. Using all of our virtues, and particularly focusing on determination, the choir took first prize in two categories and won overall.

As part of our character journey the school has engaged with the #iwill campaign. 'A key goal of the #iwill campaign is to enable organisations to understand and recognise high quality in youth social action' (Jubilee Centre 2015). Yeading Junior School was introduced to this campaign through its work with other organizations and in recognition of the strength of its youth social action. In fact, early on in our relationship with the #iwill campaign, our school was approached to feature as a case study in their publication *Transforming Young People and Communities* (Jubilee Centre 2015). Our youth social action very much aligns with the following statement in this publication: 'Youth social action is practical action in the service of others to create positive change. It provides an important mechanism for young people to develop and express their character virtues while benefiting others' (Jubilee Centre 2015). The positive change mentioned here is easily evidenced throughout our school. The case study captures the following about Yeading Junior School:

> In our school social action is not an 'add on' and our pupils know that. Children, staff, parents and governors are all involved and this whole school approach means that we inspire each other and harness the strength of like-minded people coming together. (Jubilee Centre 2015)

Schools and colleges were requested to make a pledge regarding youth social action. Alongside a number of institutions and schools, we also did so. Our #iwill Campaign Pledge states that:

> Yeading Junior School pledges to ensure that social action is at the centre of everything we do. We will campaign and participate in activities such as volunteering and fundraising encouraging support from the local community. The learning will promote resilience and inspiration. Children will become 'Agents of Change' leading the way and showing commitment to both local and global issues. We will encourage children to reflect on their actions in order to make a positive change to themselves and others.

This pledge is published on the #iwill website and is also reflected upon regularly with children, staff and governors. It is included in each headteacher's report to governors and at the time of publication, one of the co-chairs of governors stated at the end of the case study:

> Children's attitudes and values are shaped when they are young and so we cannot afford to wait until we consider them mature enough to engage in social action. We must awaken a sense of social responsibility and give them opportunities to see that what they do can and does matter. (Jubilee Centre 2015)

These virtues are evident in the language spoken daily around the school, both between the children themselves and when addressing adults. The school has been called upon to actively engage in special events. Children have spoken in wide arenas with like-minded people. In 2015, one child spoke at a WE Schools day event on the stage at Wembley Arena, London; in 2016/2017 two other children spoke many times in front of important audiences, including our own children. Through monitoring behaviour, attitude and work, it is clearly evident that character education is being embedded well and is very much part of the ethos of our whole school. In some cases, there have been good academic gains; in others, a greater focus and commitment to learning.

The school offers a huge array of extra-curricular activities. Some of our children have sung in our local community choir with other local schools and have sung for the elderly. Others take part in a range of sports. The school works closely with its local library and has engaged in a number of community projects. We have embraced a number of Team London projects. For example, through the 'Be the Best You Can Be!' programme (Mayor's Fund for London following the 2012 Olympics legacy), which promotes British Olympians and Paralympians to use the power of sports coaching to motivate and engage with young Londoners in primary and secondary schools in economically deprived areas across the capital, our children have considered their aspirations and hopes which are grounded in action and link directly to character. As Hannan from Yeading Junior School writes:

> I've been working on my Dream Folder. A Dream Folder is a book where we store all our dreams. My dream is to become a Human Rights Lawyer. I have been really inspired by Malala and Nelson Mandela who achieved their goals, which has inspired me to fulfil my dreams for the future. (Mayor's Fund for London n.d.)

Through our work with Team London, the school is now working alongside an enterprise adviser to enhance and develop the children's understanding of the qualities and skills they would need for the future. Children have taken part in yoga activities and even up-skilled one another in the art of reflection, which aligns with moral and emotional grounding.

Is leadership vision key to the success?

As Daniel Goleman (1998, p.149) states: 'Leadership is not domination, but the art of persuading people to work toward a common goal.' The development of our character virtues has been nurtured by the leadership of the school with the engagement of key role models. In its inception, it was important to ensure that these were embedded within the classroom, therefore selected teachers were requested to use the 'character codes', as they were initially known, within their everyday classroom practice. The change from the term 'codes' to 'virtues' came about through discussions with children in the first instance.

In 2016, following our application for a Department for Education (DfE) Character Award, the school was invited to the inaugural meeting of the Association of Character Education (ACE) at the Jubilee Centre, University of Birmingham. As a result of our attendance at this event and the highly commended status of our application, the school went on to think more deeply about our approach. This included researching further and looking at the work of those who are renowned in the field. Professor James Arthur from the Jubilee Centre for Character and Virtues, outlined the impact of character education on schools, stating that:

> Quite simply we know that visible and explicit character education leads students to the desire to do the right things at school and therefore leads to school success. Schools that are values-driven see character education as part of everything they do and are committed to promoting core virtues which positively links character to examination success, and more importantly, to the ideal of a flourishing life. Such schools develop and live by a core language of moral purpose which makes space to allow their students to learn about being and becoming young people of good character. The virtues that make up character enable young people to enjoy rewarding and productive lives as well as learn better, and the qualities that make up good character can be learnt and taught. (Arthur 2014, p.4)

The impact of the above can be identified in our school's 2018 short OFSTED inspection report, which states: 'Pupils behave well in lessons and around the school. They are friendly and polite, reflecting the school's 10 character virtues which the school has embedded in its ethos: resilience, teamwork, compassion, respect, volunteering, pride, curiosity, reflection, dignity and determination.' The report also cited an example of good character: 'A girl explained that new children are welcomed freely, no matter what their background or life experience. This example is typical of the thoughtful, generous and positive attitudes that pupils have.'

As work progressed, staff identified the links and approaches that had developed over time and looked at the synergy with the framework for character, as set out by the Jubilee Centre, so that children and families understood further. A new core language developed throughout the school and permeated all policies. The school sought every opportunity to share its work and activity more widely. This is demonstrated through our website, through our school's Community House for parents, parental communication and through the governing body meetings. Governors are actively involved and engage with this work. Some programmes are shared between schools in our cluster. For some of the activities, the school has bid for additional funding. Some of our work has also featured in articles and publications (e.g. financial education activities). The school took part in some work around the dangers of loan sharks and was featured on the *BBC News* website (Codd 2014). The school has also been featured in the news media (Tan 2012) for its good work in the field of financial education. Further information about our approach to financial education and literacy can be found in Chapter 7. Needless to say, following our application for a DfE Character Award, we were delighted to have been accredited with a 'highly commended' status.

A whole school approach has been taken with the abovementioned programmes. Notably, children in Year 6 were encouraged to become ambassadors and to share their learning and experiences with the rest of the school. All children are strongly encouraged to fully participate in all of the programmes. Yeading Junior School has also shared best practice with other schools within our cluster. Local programmes that bring virtue and strength to character education, such as The Mayor of London's (n.d.) 'Be the Best You Can Be' programme, are embedded within the school. Policies, a whole school vision statement and a vision statement for each class, together with the engagement of the *Rights Respecting Schools* programme (UNICEF, n.d.), have led to even wider engagement and an aspirational and flourishing community.

What has made character development even more visible has been the writing on the wall in the corridors, in the hall and subsequently in the canteen. This writing captures the list of character virtues that we focus upon. Staff, children, parents and visitors cannot fail to see these important words. A set of cards, one for each child, is available in all classrooms. Teachers give these out at the start of the day and when necessary may gently encourage children to reflect on their corporate commitment to the virtues. Through observing children's behaviour, attitudes and work, it has become evident that character education is taught well. This will be outlined in small case studies.

Through hearing from a range of inspirational speakers, children have come to an understanding that the virtues are inextricably linked and one person's journey could embody all the virtues at different junctures. To that end, the school has a naturally emerging leader amongst the 'Special Agents of Change', originally known as 'Agent Code'. Subsequently, we have shared that role amongst three very dedicated learners who embody the virtues in all aspects of their life and learning; they have also expressed a desire to develop further and deepen their understanding in all contexts. Their role and positive attitudes continue to be an inspiration for all. A visitor to the school wrote the following acknowledgement, having seen some of the children reflecting on character: 'The effect of the Agent Virtues was clear to see in the children's compassion, confidence and sense of connectedness to each other, their community and the world.' On a more recent visit, another colleague from an organization stated:

> The effort your young people and staff made for our visit was touching and I was inspired by what I saw. We are so grateful that your school embraces social action, helping others in less fortunate circumstances and developing socially conscious young people who are some of the most compassionate I've seen. (Personal communication)

The school continues to seize every opportunity to further embed the character virtues. All children are considered to be 'Agents of Change', and badges denoting this are worn by the children. Those children who lead on projects and activities wear 'Special Agent' badges.

Further evidence is available as regards the impact of the virtues through work undertaken with the school on a lunchtime project. The importance of this was that the voice of the children played a key role in bringing about some changes concerning lunchtime expectations and practice, and effective professional development was undertaken with lunchtime staff – both caterers and those supervising the children. All stakeholders became familiar with our character virtues and scripted explanations. Everyone began to speak the same language at lunchtime, which reflected the language that was used during the school day and beyond. Children were therefore receiving greater consistency in the communication of messages conveyed, which resulted in greater respect for, and integration of, lunchtime staff within the school community as well as their enhanced sense of belonging and of being valued.

Using the virtues throughout everyday life, inside and outside of school, has had a positive and profound impact on parents, their relationship with their children and their partnership with the school. Guest speakers attending the school quickly relate to the virtues emblazoned on the wall in the hall, including a Paralympian who spoke about these and related them directly back to her achievements. Virtues have been embedded in policies. We have captured comments from other schools that have visited and noticed the impact. So, what have the virtuous children of Yeading Junior School learned? A number of recent letters from children have indicated that a focus on reflection has enabled children to reconsider some of their previous actions and ways of working. One such letter stated:

I am writing to request to be a Special Agent. I think that I would be good for the role as I show all of the character virtues, also I try my best to learn how to do tasks. I have been inspired by many people including Craig and Marc Keilberger as well as the children who spoke on WE day. They have shown me what can happen if you work hard, if you try your best, if you believe in yourself and if you believe that you were born to change the world. Finally, I would like to share some ways that I have demonstrated the character virtues: I respect my teacher, I reflect on my work, I show resilience and determination in sport and I am compassionate towards others. Furthermore, I like to be very helpful and love to take social action and enjoy this within school. I would enjoy participating in campaigns such as WE ARE RAFIKIS and WE SCARE HUNGER because it would make me happy to change the planet we are living on.

The following is an extract from a discussion with six 'Agents of Change' and which was sent to #iwill as part of a blog. When asked about the impact of social action and children's voice, they responded as follows, which demonstrates that the character virtues are fully understood:

Social Action makes us feel confident and self-empowered. It makes us confident to talk to adults and give our honest opinion. Over time, we feel it has made us empathise with other people and take action for their situations. All our actions are linked together. We first find a cause where we can help others, such as homelessness. We plan our Social Action together and try to make it impactful. Then, we make it inclusive across the school. Together we carry out our Social Action. Finally, we reflect and look at the impact we have made. However, we don't stop there, we continue to raise awareness and support causes that need our help. These may affect the community or the world. We feel that when we undertake social action we are learning in a more powerful way and we can use those skills elsewhere in our learning.

This empirical evidence captures the fact that these virtues, which are discussed, enacted and studied each day, are indeed having a profound impact on teaching and learning.

Parental engagement and interest in the approach

For some significant time, since 2004, the school has established a Community House where parents can engage in programmes connected with their children's learning in school, undertake learning programmes for themselves, or simply to seek advice. The Community House is at the very heart of the school community, offering a range of inspirational opportunities for parents. It is a place of learning, friendship and partnership, where ambition flourishes. Its work has a significant impact on the whole school and fully endorses the insights advanced by Desforges:

> In the primary age range the impact caused by different levels of parental involvement is much bigger than differences associated with variations in the quality of schools. The scale of the impact is evident across all social classes and all ethnic groups. (Desforges with Abouchaar 2003)

Parents take advantage of training courses that develop their self-esteem and confidence. They share ideas that affect change. The work of the Community House has helped parents to raise expectations and has contributed to their children being successful. The Community House is a place where people celebrate culture and networks, taking pride in their local community. It is a place where we acknowledge and celebrate the richness of our community. Our Community House has given people a voice, lasting friendships, and engagement with professionals and other groups, as well as an opportunity to feel proud. Parents learn more about character education and our set of character virtues, using these to support their own behaviour management of children and to share engagement with projects in the school. In more recent times, parents have volunteered to create artefacts for whole school projects and to assist in fundraising for charity. At a recent cake sale, parents willingly donated cakes and also gave money to children to purchase cakes. The school raised the princely sum of £600 for charity.

In the research work on *The Schools for Human Flourishing*, in a section entitled 'Nurturing the heart through service learning', Dame Julia Cleverdon (2016) states: 'It became clear the greatest schools saw the purpose of education far beyond a narrow definition of academic success.

It lay as much in preparing and inspiring young people to give more and get more from their lives.' In her review, she further goes on to discuss one pupil from our school:

> Once young people have the social action bug, they become the inspiration for others. One student at Yeading Junior School, whose social action was recognised at 'WE Day', speaking to thousands of others, inspired her father to make social action a core part of what he and his colleagues do at work (cited in Desforges with Abouchaar 2003).

The child's father had explained why the children had been fundraising for sustainability, and talked about what the children had been doing. Furthermore, he introduced his colleagues to the charity online and so they too realized the importance of global social action as well as local action. The consequence was that the father brought in a significant amount of funds to support the cause. His colleagues were also very impressed with the impact this charity had on their friend's daughter and apparently this took them on the path of acting for social change. The effect on the pupil was considerable and reinforced her understanding of positive influences and teamwork.

We have observed that this 'social action bug' is extremely infectious and has also naturally evolved and grown throughout the school. In recent times, we have had staff who have contributed in their own time to displays related to projects. We have also had parents who have contributed much to support their children in volunteer activities and have been supportive in attending projects. Not only do children recognize the importance of particular activities, but so too do the parents, who frequently request for their children to take part.

What do the virtuous children of Yeading Junior School demonstrate?

Virtuous children display selfless characteristics, and over time the children learn to enhance their previously mentioned volunteering skills in a variety of ways across the school. They run clubs to support reading for newly arrived pupils. Using a variety of character virtues, some children have more recently established an after-school 'Arts and Crafts Club' to support the young girls after-school club in Ecuador. This year, a number of children attended the London Borough of Hillingdon Volunteer

Awards ceremony to receive recognition for their volunteer work with the elderly, associated with the Northwood Live at Home Scheme. In this intergenerational work, the young team engaged in weekly visits with the older residents in Northwood who were learning to access iPads in order to communicate with their families as well as to undertake daily tasks.

The school has also received a volunteer award from Team London in relation to the many aspects of volunteering the young people have undertaken, particularly through the engagement of WE Schools.

In speaking about the impact of the WE movement on the children's day-to-day learning at this celebratory event, I stated: 'The ideas and philosophy from WE Schools have supported the transformation of what's going on in school with regard to social action. Children have realized they can be empowered to make a difference and they are demonstrating that.'

Qualitative measures within school indicate the successful impact of character education on our children. Children who have spoken in front of large audiences have been tracked and continued to perform well academically; there is clear written evidence from other children that they too aspire to this 'Special Agent' role and all the qualities it embodies. They have indeed recognized the success of their peers and are keen to become 'Change Agents'. Moreover, parents of these children and their wider families have taken a greater role in different aspects of school life.

One child who had an in-year transition to the school promptly understood the vision and aims and quickly showed a very clear understanding of all the character virtues. He has played key roles in assemblies and other whole school arenas. His work showed really good progress and he became very articulate in a wide range of contexts, including the classroom. Other children and staff commented on his positive approach and his ability to influence others for good. His mother came to the school full of praise for the evident change in her son. His confidence, resilience and determination are such that he was comfortable speaking in front of adults and children alike, with little prior warning. He previously did not engage so well in school and his confidence as well as attitude to school and learning differed considerably.

Another child who spoke about her volunteering journey in a prestigious arena has settled confidently into her secondary school and has made a positive impact on her whole family. Her younger brother became a reflective learner and had the desire to emulate the work of his sister, as he saw this as a key to success. He recognized that following the character virtues was a toolbox that enabled him to achieve what he desired. He indicated this through expressing views and developing a more positive attitude as well as a work ethic. This was a tremendous success, as previously he did not approach school and learning with enthusiasm.

Our group of 'Special Agents' has grown significantly since their role was initially established, and their strong pupil voice has enabled projects and activities to flourish. They themselves have discovered new and innovative ways of harnessing support for projects and engaging key personnel who can ensure that things happen. This has been done through expressing views and opinions in writing and through group discussions. The writing of these particular children has really shown flair and skill. New creative opportunities and different avenues to explore have enabled them to research and extend their vocabulary accordingly. One of these 'Special Agents' recently stated:

> I learnt that there are people in this world right now, just like us, children around the same age as us and they don't have the same opportunities as us and are in slavery, while we are here taking things for granted and I'm at school playing and enjoying life. If we have the opportunity to help others, then we should.

A research paper by the Department for Education (2017) outlines what successful character education should look like and reflects on its importance. It recognizes that schools approach this differently according to their needs. I could identify with the section of the report below, which outlines what schools consider to be successful implementation. Key role models are certainly essential to cascade the strong ethos into every angle of school life; these strong role models emanate from all corners of our school. Within Yeading Junior School, the children have demonstrated great leadership qualities in particular and have been ceaseless advocates of what we are trying to achieve.

> Successful character education was felt to depend on a clear vision and whole school approach embedded across the curriculum. It needed to be driven forward by strong leadership and delivered and modelled by staff with the appropriate skills, time and access to activities that could be tailored appropriately to the needs of students. School staff felt that recognition needs to be given to the importance of developing Character in pupils. Resources and skills are required to support

practice in developing Character, alongside other requirements for academic success. Teachers needed to be encouraged, developed and supported with activities to develop character traits in their pupils. (DfE 2017, p.9)

Without a doubt, strong networks and partnerships have made a significant difference to the work at Yeading Junior School. These partnerships have led to the school being able to host an array of high-calibre visitors who have brought interesting aspects of their own successful journeys to the fore, enabling the children to identify qualities that have led to success. As part of our own successful journey, it has been necessary to review our team approach and to ensure that staff have appropriate training and feel supported. Clearly, our vision is to ensure that all staff are trained or mentored by others.

The school employs a number of para-professionals who form an internal Children and Families team. This team, consisting of learning mentors, a social worker and a home–school worker, has also been instrumental in working with staff, children and parents around our virtues approach. All staff are aware of the importance of using the character virtues as a means of encouraging positive behaviour and reflective and curious young learners who show Determination, Teamwork and Dignity. Furthermore, our staff are aware that using the virtues instils resilience in all its aspects, encourages mutual respect and promotes volunteering both inside and outside of school. The work on character education that threads throughout the curriculum and beyond enables children to become proud of themselves, their achievements, families and community, whilst understanding the strong impact of working as part of a team with a common purpose.

In conclusion, it is evident from the multiple comments made by visitors, parents and organizations that work with our school that the character virtues play a significant role in the everyday life and work of Yeading Junior School. Our endeavours continue in a cyclical fashion as new children, staff and parents join our strong and reflective community.

References

Arthur, J. (2014) *Being of Good Character*. Insight Series. Birmingham: The Jubilee Centre for Character and Virtues (University of Birmingham).

Berliner, W. (2017) 'Why there's no such thing as a gifted child.' *The Guardian*, 25 July. Accessed 07/05/2019 at www.theguardian.com/education/2017/jul/25/no-such-thing-as-a-gifted-child-einstein-iq

Cleverdon, J. (2016) 'Nurturing the heart through service learning.' In Church of England Education Office *The Schools for Human Flourishing*, pp.25–31. London: The National Society for the Promotion of Education, Church of England and Church in Wales, The Schools Network Ltd (SSAT) and The Woodard Corporation.

Codd, D. (2014) 'The dangers of loan sharks to be taught in schools.' *BBC News*, 3 March. Accessed 07/05/2019 at www.bbc.co.uk/news/business-26376737

Council on Social Action (CoSA) (2008) 'Side by side: A report setting out the Council on Social Action's work on one-to-one.' Paper No. 2. London: Cabinet Office & Community Links.

Department for Education (DfE) with the National Centre for Social Research (2017) *Developing Character Skills in School: Summary Report*. London: DfE.

Desforges, C. with Abouchaar, A. (2003) *The Impact of Parental Involvement, Parental Support and Family Education on Pupil Achievements and Adjustment. A Literature Review. Research Report RR433*. London: DfES.

Dhiman, S. (2015) *Ghandi and Leadership. New Horizons in Exemplary Leadership*. Basingstoke: Palgrave Macmillan.

Goleman, D. (1998) *Working with Emotional Intelligence*. London: Bloomsbury.

Jubilee Centre (2015) *#iwill Transforming Young People and Communities*. Birmingham: The Jubilee Centre for Character and Virtues (University of Birmingham).

Mayor's Fund for London (n.d.) 'Be the Best You Can Be!' Accessed 07/05/2019 at www.mayorsfundforlondon.org.uk/programme/be-the-best-you-can-be-london

Ofsted (2018) *Yeading Junior School*. Accessed 08/10/19 at https://reports.ofsted.gov.uk/provider/21/102403

Tan, C. (2012) 'Baby economics: How – and why – ten-year-olds are being taught to run a business.' *The Spectator*, 24 March. Accessed 07/05/2019 at www.spectator.co.uk/2012/03/baby-economics

United Nations International Children's Emergency Fund (UNICEF) (n.d.) *Rights Respecting Schools*. London: UNICEF. Accessed 07/05/2019 at www.unicef.org.uk/rights-respecting-schools/the-rrsa/what-is-a-rights-respecting-school

Chapter 2

Interfaith at Yeading Junior School

ELENOR PAUL

'Interfaith' is an expression which encompasses people of different faiths and religions. Interfaith in practice is the product of living in a pluralistic society and, therefore, by extension, is embedded within the everyday practices of communities, workplaces and schools. This chapter explains how Interfaith works positively and productively at Yeading Junior School both within the classroom and beyond. It demonstrates how a school-based ethos driving Interfaith faith dialogue can serve as a model of best practice which can act for the benefit of pupils, the local community and the wider society.

Interfaith

Yeading Junior School sits in the outermost western borough of London. Hillingdon is nestled between the urban boroughs of Ealing and Hounslow and the leafy counties of Berkshire and Buckinghamshire. This is pertinent, as many of our pupils move on to grammar schools that are located outside London. Hillingdon also contains Heathrow Airport, the country's global international hub. To the east of Hayes, a mere mile from the school, lies the town of Southall, notable for its Interfaith communities, whilst a few miles to the west is the conservative town of Uxbridge. Therefore, Yeading Junior School pupils are geographically exposed to a varied and diverse set of communities.

Interfaith is integral to the practices of Yeading Junior School. It happens serendipitously in every classroom, every group activity, during playtime, at lunchtime and in every assembly. It is more than a by-product of good Religious Education (RE). In the classroom, children learn from and with children from other faiths. In the canteen, children are able to eat meals which suit their dietary requirements according to their faith. In the playground, children play together regardless of background. Interfaith can play a huge role in uniting people of different faiths and encouraging children to live and work harmoniously with people of all faiths.

Yeading Junior School has a long-standing history of clarity and focus with regard to Interfaith. Interfaith always plays a huge role in the school because it is evident throughout the school and it matters to staff and pupils alike. Interfaith Week and the concept of Interfaith have been celebrated differently throughout the years and some of these achievements are explained in the following paragraphs.

In 2008, Yeading Junior School led the schools' cluster group of RE co-ordinators on a collaborative project to celebrate Interfaith. We invited pupils to create artworks to depict a religious festival. These were then used to produce a joint A3 calendar which was printed the following academic year. The RE co-ordinators were literally overwhelmed by the thousands of entries submitted and found it impossible to whittle them down to just the 12 required for each calendar month. Instead, the decision was taken to use a selection for several of the months, and the end-product was stunning. A successful bid for funding meant that every family from the five primary schools involved received a calendar, as well as all the pupils in Year 7 of the two high schools which also submitted entries. The outcomes of this project clearly demonstrated that there was a desire for cross-school Interfaith dialogue and activities. Pupils and staff in our locality were not only willing to work together to promote community cohesion but were also longing to do so. This is significant, as it exemplified that the community was receptive to initiatives which worked not only towards sharing and harmony but also towards respect, pride and teamwork, three of the character virtues that are cultivated at Yeading Junior School.

The Schools' Interfaith calendar project was the impetus for subsequent Interfaith activities which took place over the next few years. Interfaith Weeks saw many conference-style events emerging for parents and pupils from across the borough (Hillingdon People 2009, p.5). These were held at various locations within the borough, including the council's Civic Centre, a secondary school and several church halls. Themes included:

- Community Cohesion.
- Who or What Influences You?

- How Has the Olympics Created a Positive Change in the Community?
- Inequality and Faith.

These illustrious outreach events were highly popular and served the community well. They brought together adults and children who live side by side yet, hitherto, had not interacted with each other. They created shared experiences and values and fulfilled the role of 'capacity building' as defined by Cantle (2008, p.11). They also highlighted the strapline behind these events: 'Many People, Many Voices, Many Beliefs, One Community.'

Some comments captured from attendees include:

I learnt that it is really important to care and respect each other.

I learnt about teamwork in the community.

It's good to know what other people think about the community.

I made new friends. I have got an idea of how a community works.

Following the reframing of the Community Cohesion agenda, particularly since the demise of the Conservative–Liberal Democrat coalition government in England and the introduction of a new National Curriculum in 2014 (DfE, 2013), our subsequent Interfaith celebrations gave us the opportunity to reflect upon ourselves and our future direction of travel to embed a fervent and comprehensive understanding of Interfaith with our pupils.

National Interfaith Week

During Interfaith Week 2016, we invited pupils to write a message about their understanding of Interfaith that we could add to our school's 'Tree of Hope'. A snapshot of some comments made by the children within each of our year groups includes the following:

Year 3

All religions are just as important as ours and we should respect other people's religions.

We should all care about each other and treat everyone fairly.

To promote better interfaith relations, we could listen to each other.

Year 4

- No matter what religion we are, we must treat each other the same. We are all human beings.

  I hope poverty will stop and make the world a better place.

  What is important to me: to care about everyone in the world. Help the world.

Year 5

- A good way to overcome a barrier to good Interfaith relations is to be more mindful, co-operate together and join in with other religious celebrations and to be fully educated about other religions.

  Interfaith works well when some religions use empathy to understand other religions.

  My hope is we will work together to raise awareness of all religions so we can live a peaceful life.

Year 6

- Interfaith is consulting with religions with teamwork and compassion. Achieve your goals with different people around the world.

  Interfaith Week means to me that all religions are someone's belief; that everyone's equal and there should be no hate and racism in the world.

  Interfaith Week is important to me because it is one of the great ways which leads us to good communication and relationship[s] with a true person.

These comments show more than an understanding garnered via a spiral curriculum. They demonstrate the thoughts and perceptions of children, from simplistic idealistic hopes for the future to more complex condemnation of unwanted aspects of human life which are visible in society today. Through reflection, which is cultivated as a virtue at Yeading Junior School, children soon begin to understand the responsibilities they have and how they can affect others. They realize that they are empowered to work towards a vision of society, wherein inherently benevolent common goals drive people and lead us towards a community which works for the betterment of everybody.

In 2017, Yeading Junior School celebrated Interfaith with its very first Interfaith exhibition, which was held during the nationally recognized Interfaith Week. Each class worked collaboratively to produce a piece for the exhibition. Classes were tasked with linking Interfaith to one of our character virtues, and the artwork submitted was exceptional. In addition, children and families were invited to produce items for the exhibition. We were inundated with entries, which included a range of sculptures, posters, poetry and artwork. There were entries from families of all faith backgrounds and from families of no faith background. This is important because it signalled one of the first times that these families could work together creatively, exploring their beliefs and practices.

The inclusive nature of this event should not be underestimated. It allowed families for whom religion is unimportant to share their ideas of non-belief with others, thereby putting them on an equal footing with faith believers. All children and adults were invited to view the exhibition. What was originally planned as a one-day exhibition was subsequently extended to a three-day extravaganza to allow for more parents and friends of the school to visit. This very successful event showcased the willingness of our pupils and their families regarding the promotion of a cohesive community.

During Interfaith Week 2018, schools from across the London Borough of Hillingdon were invited to bring Year 5 pupils to a 'Respect for All' (UNESCO 2014) conference. This event was billed as 'a one-day RE conference to explore and express ideas about respect for all, identity and community, whoever you are!'

One hundred and nineteen pupils from 17 schools attended, as well as 29 adults. What was especially welcome was the inclusion of pupils from faith schools housed within the borough. In attendance were pupils from one Church of England School and two Sikh schools. This allowed pupils from those schools to fully integrate with other pupils within their community, with whom they might not otherwise interact. Held in the brand new Science, Technology, Engineering and Mathematics (STEM) Centre at Brunel University London, the well-behaved and polite children fully engaged with, and participated in, all of the activities with great enthusiasm. They demonstrated such profound and meaningful questioning both verbally and in written form. For example, in response to a photograph of a group of girls sitting together laughing and joking, whilst one girl sat alone in the forefront of the picture, one child asked, 'Why do they not care that she is sad and alone?' Instead of wondering what the girls were discussing, this child instinctively recognized the lonely person in the picture and chided the behaviour of those who were at best ignoring her or at worst bullying her. Immediately, the responder demonstrated an empathetic nature towards a person suffering victimization. Other questions posed by Year 5 children during the morning included:

What makes some people think they are better than others?

Why can't people compromise and make the right choice?

Why can't the world live in peace and harmony?

Why do people have to suffer in the world?

Why can't people notice homeless people, even if they aren't in a rush?

This sample of questions illustrates that children as young as 9 years of age are capable of recognizing injustice in the world. They are perfectly poised to reflect upon their place in society and to consider what they can do for the benefit of others within their community. The following questions, which they then asked, show that they want to change unwanted behaviours:

How do we grow and learn as a person?

How can we show respectful behaviour?

Here we can see that the pupils are ready, willing and keen to tackle negative actions.

A planned outcome of this day included continuing professional development (CPD) for the teachers who attended. It was an aim that staff could gather some teaching strategies in a practical manner and be able to use and develop the skills and tasks that were demonstrated. Staff and pupils were encouraged to share teaching ideas on their return to school. One pupil referred to the day as 'Epic! Best RE day ever'.

Interfaith and character virtues

The context of the staff, pupils, families and community where Yeading Junior School is located means that religion cannot be ignored. In addition to children of no faith backgrounds, our school has children from six faiths, including five of the six major faiths, and a small percentage of children who identify with other faiths, as shown in Table 2.1. Therefore, our children enter the school with varying degrees of religious practice and belief, and it is incumbent upon the school to take this into account when implementing a whole school holistic ethos which aims to nurture the virtuousness of its pupils.

Table 2.1 Pupils' religious affiliation in 2014–2015 and 2018–2019

Religion	2014–2015 (%)	2018–2019 (%)
Muslim	39	43
Hindu	26	23
Sikh	19	18
Christian	7	9
Buddhist	1	2
Other	3	2
No Religion	3	2
Roman Catholic	1	1

Note: Not all columns add up to 100 due to rounding of percentages

The statistics in Table 2.1 show that a majority of pupils affiliate themselves with a religious faith. This means they participate in religious practices and customs and have an experiential reality of religion due to their home life and upbringing. It is clear that although there has been a slight decrease in the number of Hindu pupils at the school and an increase in Muslim children since 2014–2015, the overall picture of religious membership is one of overwhelmingly religious rather than areligious as the norm.

It is therefore hugely important that knowledge of this relational context is taken into consideration when developing a programme of study that goes beyond the academic curriculum and which aims to influence the very character of pupils. As Arthur (2019) cautions, particularly in relation to the complex and multiple ways that 'character-building' has historically been interpreted over time, any 'attempt to disentangle the various elements of this conceptual relationship between the "secular" and "religious" is fraught with difficulty'. Indeed, if we are to work towards a more cohesive society, then we must strive towards positive outcomes of Interfaith such as 'building bridges rather than walls' through the promotion of 'social and religious inclusion and cohesion' (McCowan 2017).

Interfaith beyond the school gates

Yeading Junior School has led a group of cluster schools in working collaboratively to promote community cohesion throughout the Hayes area. Part of this work resulted in two innovative Interfaith events involving children from nine schools within the group. During these conferences the children participated in a range of interactive and fun activities that enabled them to share ideas, learn new skills and work towards cohesion within the community.

These events resulted in similar events taking place back in each school environment, which saw thousands of children using the Interfaith event theme 'Working together with others' in order to provide services for others. Feedback from schools demonstrated an increased awareness for others, and many schools held large-scale fundraising activities to improve the living conditions of many people around the world. As an example, we at Yeading Junior School made and donated over 300 hospital gowns that, in turn, saved the hospitals concerned enough money to pay for operations to repair the cleft palates of six children, which is life-changing.

Following on from this work, an Interfaith community event was extended to include parents. The theme for this event was also entitled 'Working together with others' and focused on recognizing and celebrating the differences amongst people; at the same time, it allowed community members to see that 'others' are just like themselves. The aim was to bring together a group of people simply to understand a little more about people for whom, without this event, they would never even think of getting to know. This was a highly successful evening, wherein parents and their children from across the schools met together to participate in activities to promote community cohesion.

When asked what they had learned from the event, some participants stated:

A good idea for pupils to meet children from other schools.

A great opportunity to meet others from different cultures and to see what other schools in the area are doing.

I have made new friends and enjoyed being part of the community.

I was able to meet parents of other children and learned from their diverse backgrounds.

I made new friends. I have got an idea of how a community works.

We came to know about people living in our area which we didn't know.

I learned something new about other people.

Talking to people for the first time is good – sharing thoughts, ideas and beliefs.

Some of the evaluative statements gathered from participants included:

I strongly recommend that this event continues. It is helpful to the community.

It was fun for me and my child. Thank you for your time to organize this event.

Please arrange this type of event at least 3–4 times a year, as it is so much fun for kids, and parents as well.

This event may have encouraged other people to learn about others and understand them.

I hope these kinds of events expand to further communities, not just schools.

It is nice to have events like this again.

These events show that Interfaith activities are not only valuable but are also highly valued. They highlight the need for Interfaith dialogue to be planned and facilitated in order for such opportunities to work effectively. Furthermore, these events demonstrate the importance of Interfaith dialogue between members of the community by the members of that community. This is vital as it validates, in the eyes of the pupils, the message about good relations as it is being espoused both at home and in school.

Interfaith and the curriculum

Interfaith can be explored through RE lessons. RE and Interfaith encompass many facets of learning which are immeasurable. Architects of an RE curriculum have argued that an aim of RE is to promote community cohesion (Buckinghamshire RE Agreed Syllabus 2011–2016; Ealing Agreed Syllabus of Religious Education 2014; Hillingdon Religious Education Syllabus 2017) and to prepare pupils to live in the wider world (Hillingdon Religious Education Syllabus 2017: London Borough of Hounslow 2016; Pan Berkshire Agreed Syllabus for Religious Education 2018–2023). Indeed, the UK government declares this to be a fundamental aim of education (DfE 2013).

In relation to our own specific context, the purpose and entitlement behind the Hillingdon Religious Education Syllabus has been expressed as follows:

> Religious Education is an important facet of Hillingdon's young people's education as it informs our students about how religious beliefs, embedded in a vast array of faiths, provides the underpinning for the ways people live their lives and provides a significant contribution to their decision making with regard to right and wrong action. Given this, the study of religion both in terms of its content and its enactments is crucial to the achievement of an educated person in Hillingdon today.
>
> RE can thus make a fundamental contribution to community cohesion, citizenship and spiritual, moral, social and cultural development. Nevertheless, children and young people must have also an understanding of what it is to be someone of no religious faith. Furthermore, the fact that the locally agreed syllabus is produced with the involvement of all aspects of the local community and its schools, including those that are not tied to the locally agreed syllabus, helps ensure that it supports community cohesion, including inter-faith working.
>
> RE equips pupils with the skills to understand and explain the human values which are shared between religious and other worldviews. They learn to weigh up the value of wisdom from different sources, to develop and express their insights in response and to agree or disagree respectfully. To achieve this RE must be taught in an objective and pluralistic manner, and not as indoctrination into a particular faith or belief.
>
> Teaching RE should foster and develop key discernment skills including interpreting, understanding and evaluating texts, the knowledge in the selection of authoritative texts and critical

thinking skills. This will lead to a high level of religious literacy among our young people with the skills to participate positively in our contemporary society. (Hillingdon RE Syllabus 2017, pp.1–2)

When teaching RE, an Aristotelian view of education may be required. This aim seeks to position the child and their understanding of themselves and the world at the core and forefront of education. Thus, an outcome of teaching in this manner could lead to pupils better able to lead lives in society which promote the good of mankind. This stance is required when aiming to nurture and develop virtuous children whose social, cultural, religious and financial backgrounds are so diverse and varied.

A further aim of RE is to develop religiously literate pupils. This outcome of RE places the subject, and rightly so, as equal to other subjects, worthy of study and listed in the National Curriculum. Its purpose is for learners to understand the complex nature of religion and how it is lived out by its followers. RE provides a platform wherein discussion and reflection of religious beliefs and practices can be discussed openly and platonically, without prejudice. This becomes apparent in the daily lives of our children when aspects of good Interfaith dialogue are spontaneously demonstrated.

RE can be taught according to Jerome Bruner's (1960) model of a spiral curriculum in which 'there is an iterative revisiting of topics, subjects or themes throughout the course. A spiral curriculum is not simply the repetition of a topic taught. It requires also the deepening of it, with each successive encounter building on the previous one' (Harden 1999). As RE is a statutory school subject, teachers can transfer the skills learned to teach RE to aid in the implementation of character virtues, which could allow topics to be revisited and, each time, a deeper and more meaningful understanding would be gained.

Yeading Junior School's impetus for developing character virtues can, and does, revisit themes and ideologies in a similar manner to that of a spiral curriculum, so that the children grow and deepen their understanding. An example of this can be recognized in the following narrative:

As part of a unit of work in RE, the children in Year 5 learned about the Third Pillar of Islam – *zakat* (alms). Later in the year, the same children also learned about the Buddhist practice of the alms bowl and how it enables monks to survive. This learning coincided with a fundraising event, held on one particular day, when children were invited to share and celebrate the good that they have done in school or in the community. During this day, which saw children reaffirm their desire to make a difference in the world, each class was tasked with designing and carrying out an activity that supported the school's vision 'to be the change' the children wanted to see. Whilst some classes created beautiful items to sell in their effort to raise funds, other classes provided services for others in exchange for their donations to charity. Furthermore, those Year 5 children who had fully engaged in the RE lessons opted to promote and run a charitable drive, in the form of a book swap. They invited children to donate books they no longer needed and to swap them for ones they wanted. In return, the children requested that a small financial contribution be made, which would then be amassed and donated to the nominated charity. The event was highly successful and raised a three-figure sum. One year later, these same children chose to run the book swap again. They once more collected a huge number of books and raised a large sum of money for charity. There was however a noticeable shift in their attitude from their request for books to their sales patter. Their attitude to charity had veered from one using charity selfishly – as somewhere to dump your unwanted items – toward one that was far more benevolent. The children started to think of charity, almost as a self-sacrifice, as they had developed an understanding that giving up something valuable to you is far more virtuous than simply giving away something that you did not really want in the first place. Ideals that are supported by the religious practices of *langar*,[1] *zakat*,[2] tithing and the Buddhist notion of interdependence. The children pleaded: 'Please bring in books that you think other children will want to read, books that you have liked so that others can enjoy them too.' They were also more compassionate when redistributing the books, as this exchange reveals: 'You've only got 20p? That's OK. I can see that you really want this book, and you're giving to charity so I'm giving to you. Here, you can have it.'

This brief anecdote is but one example of how Bruner's spiral curriculum model can be applied to the themes explored within RE. It shows how children are able to reflect upon the beliefs and attitudes of others and

---

1   *Langar,* is the term used in Sikhism for the community kitchen in a *Gurdwara* (place of worship), where a free meal is served to all the visitors, without distinction of religion, caste, gender, economic status or ethnicity. The free meal is always vegetarian.

2   *Zakat* is a form of alms giving, which is treated in Islam as a religious obligation or tax and by Quranic ranking is next after prayer in importance. As one of the Five Pillars of Islam, *zakat* is a religious obligation for all Muslims who meet the necessary criteria of wealth.

apply the facets they themselves find virtuous to their own thoughts and actions.

In 2018, we were accredited the Gold Quality Mark in Religious Education (REQM) from the Religious Education Council of England and Wales, which:

> recognizes high quality RE, particularly those schools which are providing their learners with authentic experiences and contributing to whole school outcomes. RE makes a powerful contribution to young people's learning. It provides them with the chance to explore the big ideas of religion and belief and think about what matters in their own lives. (RECEW n.d.)

Following our success in gaining this recognition, it was imperative to cascade good practice with teachers and schools within the borough. An important aim for RE is for the subject to be engaging. The conference we planned helped to fulfil this aim for a wider audience by providing a platform for staff to network and participate in first-class RE teaching which incorporated thoughtful, discerning, lively and stimulating strategies and discussion. When taught in this way, RE can work alongside character education to support and strengthen its benefits and outcomes.

Curiosity and Interfaith in practice

Curiosity is underpinned by wanting to know, understand and learn about others and wondering about people's thoughts, attitudes, actions and activities. An example of how curiosity is nurtured and developed within RE can be explained as follows:

> During the week when the festival of Diwali was celebrated by millions of people throughout the world, the Year 3 children were studying a unit of work on Hinduism. Due to the foresight in planning by the teachers, children were able to study the festival of Diwali in their classrooms. The timing of this lesson is important since, given the locality of the school, it was evident that children would be exposed to the festival as they would have witnessed the festivities taking place in their neighbourhood because both Hindu and Sikh families used fireworks to celebrate the Festival of Lights. Thus, the timely learning in school helped the children to understand what was taking place in the area

in which they live. Being at home allowed the children to either ignore, witness or participate in the celebrations. Being at school enabled the children to learn about, share, question and understand the meaning behind the festival. Part of the work the children were involved in was the creation of their own divas (e.g. clay pots used to hold candles that were lit during the festival) in order to externalize their learning. However, further learning ensued when they took home the items they had created so diligently. This, in many instances, sparked conversations at home about what they were studying in school. It took the learning home so that those who may have ignored the festival could explain and acknowledge its importance to their family members. Those who had witnessed the festival could encourage other family members to have a better understanding of Diwali, whilst those who celebrated Diwali felt a sense of pride and reaffirmation.

This is just one example of how one lesson, on one particular day, goes some way to develop and promote curiosity within children in order for them to have a better understanding of the people who live and study in their community, which, in turn, allows them to internalize and develop virtuous attitudes.

Yeading Junior School aims to promote and encourage parents to form relationships with people for whom, without the school, they would not ordinarily engage. The school (and, by extension, the Community House) represents a diverse pluralistic society and is a place and safe space in which questions about the 'other' can be freely asked and answers garnered so that the 'other' can be more fully understood. Whilst teachers are knowledgeable in their understanding of RE through training and CPD, the Community House has served, and continues to serve, as an invaluable source of wealth for our ancillary staff, who develop their knowledge of people of other faiths through discussions, observations and experience. Through curiosity, Interfaith dialogue produces people who fully understand their neighbours and communities, which prepares them for life.

Whole school Interfaith

Respect is an important element of being human. It is encompassed within the fundamental British values that all schools in England have been expected to promote since their introduction in 2014 (DfE 2014). Respect emerges from an understanding of others. Shared values and beliefs are borne out, albeit via different practices. Respect can only be garnered when an understanding of the 'other' has been explored and developed.

Assemblies play an important role in the life of Yeading Junior School. Collective gatherings are a time when the themes explored within RE and character education can be shared on a corporate level. This reinforces the significance of virtuous behaviour in children's daily lives. The children perform assemblies, which might share a religious story or a specific festival. Classes put on assemblies and, in so doing, demonstrate their understanding and exploration of how they implement the character virtues into their lives both in school and beyond, within their families and the wider community.

Christmas productions from all faiths are firm favourites. Every year, at the end of the Michaelmas term, Year 3 and Year 5 children produce theatrical extravaganzas. These shows are performed solely by the children and to packed audiences on each night of the performances. This illustrates the support and commitment of our families in the educational endeavours of Yeading Junior School. Over the years, these shows have included theatrical examples of the Nativity, traditional pantomimes and stories set during the festive period both at home and abroad. During the planning and rehearsing of these shows, staff work hard to ensure that children fully understand the themes of the stories. They strive to ensure that the scripts and songs are as inclusive as possible, which is a further example of seeing Interfaith in action.

Similarly, the use of religious stories can inspire our children. For example, food and toiletry items which were given during Harvest were donated to the Hillingdon Foodbank and Salvation Army collections. By linking these Christian ideals with the Sikh notion of *sewa*, or the Islamic idea of *zakat*, or by simply having empathy and compassion for others, we see children fully get behind fundraising drives which support our very own local community. Thus, good Interfaith in practice can be a catalyst for the promotion of community relations, by springboarding ideals with a strong moral bedrock, which leads to ethical virtuous behaviour.

Interfaith at Yeading Junior School has travelled a journey. Along this road, pupils have demonstrated a desire to work harmoniously with others. They have shown that they understand religious difference and they respect people's right to live and work according to their beliefs. The addition of character virtues has led to the journey being a more pleasant and insightful road to travel along. The school's approach to character virtues complements the ethos and practice of Interfaith. The skillsets that are nurtured are interchangeable between both the development of Interfaith and character virtues. All of this goes some way to preparing pupils to effectively deal with their lives outside school, both now and in the future.

References

Arthur, J. (2019) 'Christianity and the character education movement 1897–1914.' *History of Education 48*(1), 60–76.

Bruner, J. (1960) *The Process of Education*. Cambridge, MA: Harvard University Press.

Buckinghamshire RE Agreed Syllabus (2011–2016) 'Challenging RE.' Accessed 08/10/19 at https://democracy.buckscc.gov.uk/documents/s19820/DLES17.11%20Agreed%20Syllabus

Cantle, T. (2008) *Community Cohesion: A New Framework for Race and Diversity* (Revised and Updated Edition). Basingstoke: Palgrave Macmillan.

Department for Education (DfE) (2013) *The National Curriculum in England: Key Stages 1 and 2 Framework Document*. Reference: DFE-00178-2013. London: DfE.

Department for Education (DfE) (2014) *Promoting Fundamental British Values as Part of SMSC in Schools: Departmental Advice for Maintained Schools*. Accessed 20/05/19 at https://assets.publishing.service.gov.uk/government/uploads/system/uploads/attachment_data/file/380595/SMSC_Guidance_Maintained_Schools.pdf

Ealing Agreed Syllabus of Religious Education (2014) *Sowing the Seeds of the Future: An Exploration of Human Beliefs and Values*. Accessed 20/05/19 at www.egfl.org.uk/elp-services/teaching-and-learning/curriculum/curriculum-subjects/religious-education

Harden, R. M. (1999) 'What is a spiral curriculum?' *Medical Teacher 21*(2), 141–143.

Hillingdon People (2009) *News from Your Council May–June 2009*. London: London Borough of Hillingdon.

Hillingdon Religious Education Syllabus (2017). Accessed 20/05/19 at https://modgov.hillingdon.gov.uk/documents/s37670/1%20Hill%20Rev%20Syll%202017%20Rev%20Support.pdf

London ,Borough of Hounslow (2016) *Widening Horizons: The Agreed Syllabus for Religious Education in the London Borough of Hounslow*. Accessed 20/05/19 at democraticservices.hounslow.gov.uk

McCowan, T. (2017) 'Building bridges rather than walls: Research into an experiential model of interfaith education in secondary schools.' *British Journal of Religious Education 39*(3), 269–278.

Pan-Berkshire Agreed Syllabus for Religious Education 2018–2023 (n.d.). Accessed 20/05/19 at https://thelink.slough.gov.uk/news/pan-berkshire-agreed-syllabus-religious-education-2018-2023

Religious Education Council of England and Wales (n.d.) *RE Quality Mark*. Accessed 20/05/19 at www.religiouseducationcouncil.org.uk/?s=RE+Quality+Mark

United Nations Educational, Scientific and Cultural Organization (UNESCO) (2014) *Teaching Respect for All: Implementation Guide*. Paris: UNESCO.

Chapter 3

Language Learning and Acquisition

JEAN-MICHEL BALLAY

The story of language learning and acquisition featured within this chapter is set against the national policy landscape, particularly the introduction of compulsory language teaching in primary schools across England in 2014 (DfE 2012). The emergence of Latin through the successful funding of the Classics for All project in 2013, exemplifies not only forward thinking and the uniqueness of this offer to our school but also, more importantly, its very inclusive nature through 'stimulating the able and improving the literacy of the less able, and helping all pupils appreciate the West's astonishing cultural and historical inheritance from the Romans' (Classics for All 2013).

Beyond stimulating the most able and improving the literacy of the less able, the teaching of Latin has been a great catalyst in developing a sense of place and identity for all children regardless of their abilities, and each child has plunged into the task with fervour. It has broadened their understanding of language intricacies and it has allowed everyone to become language detectives. Children have had to use some of our school virtues to explore the linguistic intricacies and, by doing so, their very own character has grown exponentially. Furthermore, and beyond the linguistic gains, their sense and awareness of place has equally expanded, and children are now developing into global citizens, respectful of each other's culture and looking forward to becoming citizens of the world.

How French and Latin came to be at Yeading Junior School

Not surprisingly, any journey is set within a particular context and/or landscape, and each landscape has many layers to explore. As such, and although this is certainly not the aim of this narrative, the story of language learning and acquisition is set against a national backdrop and in particular the introduction of compulsory language teaching in Key Stage 2.

In September 2014, compulsory language teaching in primary schools across England was introduced (DfE 2012) and this certainly and undoubtedly changed the whole language landscape for many schools across the land. Where once we used to have an uncertain and arid linguistic terrain, with schools either deciding to offer languages or not, we soon saw the emergence of green linguistic shoots throughout the United Kingdom, thanks to this initiative. In fact, 'the introduction of compulsory language teaching in Key Stage 2 has had an immediate impact on the number of primary schools teaching a language. Almost all schools responding to the survey (99%) now do so and 12 per cent have just started in the current academic year (2014/2015)' (Board and Tinsley 2015, p.6). This statement clearly demonstrates that this initiative was the catalyst for a new linguistic implementation across the primary sector and a resurgence in the interest for learning and acquiring an additional language at a young age. On this note, Yeading Junior School, along with many other schools, had already been offering French or other languages long before the initiative was kickstarted, as this was in direct relation to the vision of the headteacher.

This narrative is not about commenting on the virtues of learning a second language, nor is it about the theoretical background attached to it, but rather an exploration of how language teaching and learning has come to be in our school. This linguistic journey is part and parcel of our school; it is set within our own contextual environment (e.g. locality, ethnicity, economic and social settings). It does not seek to represent a model for other schools to emulate, nor is it a recipe for success. Rather, this linguistic enterprise represents a very successful story on how languages came to be in our school, which may serve to inspire other schools seeking to promote language learning and acquisition within their own unique contexts.

How French is taught at our school

When I first arrived here, eight years ago, class teachers were the ones teaching language lessons in class with the use of a computer programme, where planning and delivery could be undertaken by a non-specialist language teacher. That programme, which is still being used today, covers 24 language units, as was then prescribed by the government (DfES 2002). These units cover a wide range of in-situ language topics and scenarios, as you would encounter them in a real-life situation, were you to travel to a French-speaking area of the world. The programme covers numerous topics, such as greetings and leisure activities, sports, food, asking for directions and so forth. It also clearly links the purely linguistic components to the cultural dimension. For instance, some units of language will be associated with a particular French-speaking part of the world, such as Martinique in the Caribbean or French Guyana in South America.

These areas of the curriculum are there to guide teachers on what linguistic aspect needs to be covered, yet this approach is in no way restrictive. Teachers can easily adapt lessons to suit their class environment and do so efficiently so as to better serve the needs of the communities represented in their respective classes. We soon, as a school, progressively moved away from being reliant on a computer programme to something which could be deemed much more substantial. This is not to say that relying on such a programme was not beneficial, but it certainly limited the language scope as a lot of the delivery had to be based on either the content of the programme itself or the subject knowledge of each individual teacher delivering the language lesson. The presence of a specialist teacher of modern foreign languages hence added another layer to the possibilities of linguistic content and delivery within our school.

French was delivered across all four of our year groups and each class would benefit from one whole hour of French teaching and learning each week. Class teachers would be asked to regularly recycle the language introduced, and all would be informed as to what language unit needed to be revisited during the week. This allowed the knowledge and understanding to be reviewed regularly and language acquisition would then be assessed at regular intervals by the specialist teacher. For instance, if the topic studied during the French lesson was about the weather and what the weather was like on a particular day, the class teacher would ask his or her class the question in French and the children had to respond in the target language (e.g. '*Quel temps fait-il aujourd'hui?*' '*Aujourd'hui il pleut/il fait beau/il y a du vent*'), which respectively translates as 'What's the weather like today?'

'Today, it's raining/it's nice weather/it's windy.' On other occasions, and within the context of a science class, the names of the planets in our solar system will also be recycled in French, as this constitutes an integral part of the French curriculum. Registers can also be taken in French, so that instead of simply saying 'present', the words or short sentences learned can be recycled at that time. In fact, there are many moments throughout the day when the class teacher can recycle part of the language learned during the language session. These short bursts of language use often prove to be more effective for language learning and acquisition than one whole hour of continuous immersion in the target language.

We also have tied in some of the French usage to other areas of the curriculum, and, on one occasion, speaking French was completely part and parcel of the financial education that we undertake here at Yeading Junior School. For example, as children went to the hall to buy different items with their Yeadoes (school currency, as detailed in Chapter 7), those who could communicate and carry out the conversation in French would benefit from a 20 per cent discount. Needless to say, most of the children were very eager to try out their linguistic skills, as they quickly realized that they could buy more things by making some effort. In this instance, it was after listening to the children's recommendations that the decision was made, which in itself, clearly shows that if as adults, we pay attention to children's voices, this can lead towards implementing new activities or looking at things in an entirely different way. When they were buying things in French and asking for the prices, it was with an immense sense of pride for a job well done.

Soon French, and to a lesser degree Spanish (since Spanish was initially introduced as a club on a Friday afternoon and suffice it to say that many pupils enrolled in this particular club), became lessons to look forward to. Pupils were indeed looking forward to their linguistic challenges and some even offered to organize their very own French club over lunchtime for Year 3, so that these younger children could get a head start in their studies. Some Year 6 children would actually teach the pupils in Years 3 and 4 the intricacies of French and Spanish. What was even more surprising was the realization that many new children coming to Year 3 from Year 2 would already start with some basic French. You would almost think that they had been exposed to French lessons in Year 2; however, that was not the case and it had never been. This raises the question: Where did they learn their French? I was soon to discover that the linguistic baggage (i.e. the knowledge, skills and understanding they came with) had actually been taught to them by their siblings, who had already been at our school for a number of years. This was certainly an epiphany and a moment of intense satisfaction, as it implied that the lessons taught in school were redelivered at home by the children themselves. It clearly demonstrated their curiosity towards learning a new language, pride in what they were capable of achieving, determination in their language learning and acquisition and in transmitting this knowledge to their younger siblings, as well as, finally, volunteering themselves to support others in their thirst for linguistic knowledge and new discoveries.

Most children at our school are polyglots. In fact, Yeading Junior School has a total number of 42 different languages spoken at home, which means that many children are regularly exposed to bilingualism or multilingualism. In other words, they already have a linguistic mind and are more often than not showing a keen interest for languages, no matter what the language might be. Undoubtedly, this constitutes an effective platform to tap into, as many of our pupils are passionate about language learning.

Beyond the language itself, the children are also very interested in learning about other cultures and their customs as the school already has a richly diverse community. This willingness to acquire a new mode of expression has been exemplified throughout our school (e.g. through role plays, assemblies and the casual recycling of the language learned in class and transferred outside the classroom and into the corridors). In fact, and in relation to the latest language research financed by the British Council, we perfectly exemplify the 40 per cent of 'schools with high proportions of pupils with English as an Additional Language, which are less likely to see this implementation as a challenge in relation to the teaching of new languages than are those with more monolingual pupil populations' (Board and Tinsley 2015, p.92).

How we added a cultural dimension to French

As French has always constituted an important dimension to our school and curriculum, and as pupils from across all of our year groups have learned it with passion and commitment, we soon added another layer to our offer by finding a partner school in France. The way we went about finding a school was indeed very straightforward. For anyone interested in doing so, all a school needs to do is either approach their own local authority, or better still, address the French Consulate directly and ask for the person in charge of education and schools to provide a list of schools one can approach, depending upon which class one is interested in and for how long.

Within a few months we successfully managed to find a French school that was willing to fully participate in the enrichment of our commitment to language learning. We have since then organized overseas trips to visit our partner school and every year we send about 32 children from Year 6 to spend the day at our partner school in Paris. We leave early in the morning and make the journey across the English Channel via Eurostar to visit our partner school. We spend most of the morning visiting landmarks, and the rest of the day is spent with the French children at their school. As they arrive in Paris, our children are immediately paired up with their French friends and are encouraged to participate actively in this linguistic exchange. Our children all come back enthused about their experience abroad and they certainly want to pursue languages as they transfer to their secondary school. They all look back on their day in Paris as a positive linguistic and cultural experience, even more so as many of the children attending this trip would not necessarily have ventured further afield than the Borough of Hillingdon, in West London. Needless to say, upon their return, their heads are buzzing with memories which they will never forget. This might even encourage them to continue their language studies at the General Certificate of Secondary Education (GCSE) level and beyond. I have had former pupils reporting back to me that they had taken languages for their GCSE precisely because the language lessons they experienced during their primary school education had been exciting, interesting and inspirational.

It is to be noted at this point that many of the children who take part in our trip to France are either Special Educational Needs (SEN) children or those eligible for Pupil Premium. For our SEN children, language learning has always been a very positive experience. They generally look at the experience of learning a new language as a positive endeavour. As language units can easily be reviewed and assimilated over time, they do not feel under pressure and none have ever been placed in a situation of failure. They look at this subject as something new where they can indeed excel, and they usually do. As one pupil once reported it to me, 'the more languages you know, the brainier you get'. In fact, 'teachers see the teaching of a new language as a leveller, in which progress is constrained neither by a low level of English nor Special Educational Needs' (Board and Tinsley 2015, p.79).

Our partner school also comes to visit us on an annual basis for two days, with an overnight stay in a nearby hotel. It will usually be a group of 22 CM2 children, equivalent to our Year 6. On their first day, our children go and greet them at St Pancras International station in central London, with banners welcoming them to England. As they come out from passport control, our children then start singing songs in French that all of the French children would be familiar with, to the amusement of other passengers as they walk by. We then go for a sightseeing tour of the major landmarks in London, followed by a nice lunch in a park. The latter part of the afternoon is spent visiting our school. The following day, our French partners are dispatched to classes across the school, where they mix with their English counterparts. The whole experience is one of mutual respect and dedication to making them feel welcome. Additionally, all of the children benefit from intercultural learning and it raises their awareness of different educational traditions and approaches to schooling.

This year, our partner school decided to make a short video about its classes, playground and canteen and this was sent to us with the best possible wishes for Christmas. We plan to return the favour to them by either doing something similar or doing some other special project to present our school. When the French video was shown to the British children, they immediately picked up on the diversity of the children and the fact that the French children did not have to wear a uniform. This provided our Year 6 class with an interesting platform for discussion and debate about cultural differences and diversity. These kinds of cultural exchanges, although simple enough to recreate, certainly provide another dimension to teaching and learning and undoubtedly reinforce the virtues of pride, respect, and compassion: pride in the work that children do for others, the respect they show for their own cultural background and that of others, and curiosity about other cultural groups and their societal differences.

To extend our partnership even further, the French local authority decided to send us a young French teacher for a year, under the banner of the programme Jules Verne. This programme is valid for one year and it allows a teacher, who will eventually be teaching English lessons to his or her class in France, to further develop his or her linguistic skills in English whilst also providing additional hours of French teaching and learning to the host school.[1] However, it is worth noting at this point that although

---

1   For further information about the Jules Verne programme, please visit eduschol.education. fr/cid52924/programme-jules-verne.html

Erasmus+² and programmes such as Jules Verne are immensely beneficial in the sense that they can provide schools with additional resources by sending native speakers to different primary schools in Europe and further afield to European overseas territories, circumstances might very well change in the future due to the uncertainties surrounding England's relationship with Europe. For example, the aftermath of Brexit may lead governments to redefine and reshape the very nature of these programmes. Whether they will continue in a different form or simply disappear altogether has yet to be determined.

A large number of children who are part of the SEN cohort also attend our Spanish and French clubs. Although this might be surprising to some readers, all of our SEN pupils have expressed how much they were looking forward to their language lessons, to the point that these lessons have almost become a necessity rather than a chore they have to complete. Many of these children would become really unsettled if the lessons did not happen – they all look forward to them. Some have even organized clubs for the younger ones, under the supervision of the specialist teacher, which include some kind of assessment carried out by the children themselves. All of this pupil-driven delivery has been carried out with passion and determination – passion for the subject and languages, and determination to accomplish the task. Progress has also been remarkable for a large majority of our SEN pupils.

The teaching of French (and to a lesser extent Spanish) has been hugely successful across our school. Our pupils have indeed exceeded all expectations. When children were assessed in their linguistic knowledge and verbal communication, they performed above the norm or national expectations. The impact of the deliveries has equally been significant at different levels. First and foremost, our children have developed a real passion for Modern Foreign Languages (MFL) and this passion can certainly be seen throughout our school and in all year groups. Second, many of our Year 3 children already come with a basic understanding of French and of how the language works, thanks to the input of their siblings at Yeading Junior School. Progress has consistently been good in MFL,

---

2   Erasmus+ is the EU programme in the fields of education, training, youth and sport for the period 2014–2020. Education, training, youth and sport can make a major contribution to help tackle socio-economic changes, the key challenges that Europe will be facing until the end of the decade, and to support the implementation of the European policy agenda for growth, jobs, equity and social inclusion. For details, please visit: https://ec.europa.eu/programmes/erasmus-plus/programme-guide/introduction/how-to-read-programme-guide_en

and many children have continued their remarkable linguistic journey into secondary school and taken GCSEs in a range of languages. Finally, parents at Yeading Junior School are ambitious for their children and see language learning as part of the educational basis for advancement in life (Board and Tinsley 2015). As a pupil once said, 'My parents are taking some tuition', and the parent's response was 'My daughter knows some French, so we should too.'

How Latin came to be introduced in our school

This section focuses on the emergence of Latin within our school and of how it slowly but surely transformed the language scene at Yeading Junior School. It all began with a vision for the school and a real passion for the subject. However, passion alone is not sufficient unless you have the funds and resources to see the project and vision through. Hence, and after some mutual understanding on all parts, the headteacher and I, as the specialist language teacher, applied for a grant of £1,000 to finance the whole project with Classics for All (CfA).

CfA is a non-profit registered charity which raises funds so that every primary and secondary state school pupil (many in areas of high deprivation) may have the opportunity to study Classics: 'The study of Classics – Latin, Ancient Greek, Classical Civilization and Ancient History – offers pupils a unique educational, intellectual and cultural experience' (CfA 2013, p.2). In 2013, this grant covered 57 schools and colleges around the United Kingdom, and it was designed to provide a launchpad for the subject, allowing it to become embedded and sustained thereafter in schools. This particular grant is offered over two to three years, which allows a sufficient amount of time for schools to launch their programmes.

It is without a doubt that we as a school – teachers, parents and pupils alike – take great pride in the fact that we are further developing our language learning and acquisition opportunities for our children through the teaching of Latin.

I would like to come back to the notion of 'uniqueness', as this word stands at the very core of what we do here at Yeading Junior School. For many decades, the teaching of Latin has been the preserve of independent schools and we certainly wanted to offer this chance to our children. It is far from being the norm to teach Latin in state schools and certainly less so within a primary setting. Therefore, we looked at this fact as just another justification and opportunity to introduce Latin into our school, and we have had no regrets about this ever since. Yeading Junior School is certainly unique within the London Borough of Hillingdon when it comes to having the option to study Classics. The second reason for us wanting to teach Latin has a great deal to do with the aforementioned quote: 'stimulating the able and improving the literacy of the less able, and helping all pupils appreciate the West's astonishing cultural and historical inheritance from the Romans' (CfA 2013, p.3).

Additionally, when you start to look at the intricacies and complexities of the English language and investigate how English has been influenced over many centuries, you start to realize that one of the best possible combinations of languages for children to have is that of French and Latin. Let's not forget that close to 59 per cent of the vocabulary making up English can be traced back to either French or Latin. For instance, words like 'brunette', 'critique', 'déjà vu', 'toilette', 'voyage', 'bouquet' and 'cliché' stem from French. In the case of Latin, one could think of such word derivations from '*lingua*' (which changed into 'language', 'lingual' and 'linguistics'), '*nauta*' (which evolved into 'nautical', 'nautilus'), and '*schola*' (from which words like 'school' and 'scholastic' emerged). As a matter of fact, when looking at the number of Latin derivatives present in English, the reader would soon begin to realize that this is a very substantial list indeed. In other words, when you start off on your linguistic journey through French and Latin, it also becomes a reflection on the development of English itself through the centuries, and that surely is worth investing in.

Beyond the languages themselves, this is also an historical and cultural journey through time and place The combination of French and Latin helps our pupils to better understand the origins of the culture they live in and the language they speak and learn on a regular basis. The study of French and Latin thus adds a valuable dimension to their learning. Many of our children certainly now look at the etymology of the words that they are learning in class in English to find out whether they originate from Latin or French. They now have a deeper understanding of how languages work and change over time. Equally, they also have an historical dimension and a sense of place that they did not have before. They have more or less become language detectives and are very much aware of how languages work. Hence, we have also changed the wording of our MFL policy and it has now become 'French and Latin, Teaching Languages with a Linguistic Approach'.

How Latin is actually taught in our school

Depending on the year group, Latin is taught either as a whole one-hour session or a half-hour session alongside French. All sessions cover a linguistic and grammatical point, side by side, with an historical and cultural aspect. The method used is one that has been developed by Cambridge University and it has always been viewed as an efficient and reliable resource. We use two of their textbooks – *Minimus* (Bell 2000) and *Minimus Secundus* (Bell 2004) – each of which has 12 language units to be covered.

Alongside the language comes a series of historical and cultural facts, which clearly adds another dimension to the texts and dialogues. They also provide a series of Roman and Greek myths, which certainly contribute to the wider development of literacy among our children. All children have looked at this experience with pride, commitment and determination. In fact, many would be utterly disappointed if they were not to receive their Latin lessons.

The story of Latin at Yeading Junior School is one of success, regardless of abilities and performance. Pupils have undertaken this journey through time and space with determination and an immense sense of pride. One of the CfA patrons, Deborah Hughes, could not have expressed it better:

> Apart from the sheer joy that the intimate study of Latin brings, it also carries with it a truly invigorating internationalist value. By allowing the next generation access to this wealth, let's hope we are remembered as an age that chose to open rather than close minds. (CfA 2013)

Opening new horizons is what Yeading Junior School is all about.

How we aim to teach linguistic skills rather than the language per se

In order to facilitate pupils' transition to secondary school, when it comes to the teaching and learning of languages, we have as a school adopted an approach where linguistic skills are considered to be more important than the language taught, in and of itself.

In essence, many of the children have come back to us over the years complaining that once they transitioned to secondary schools they were given a different language to study in Year 7 rather than capitalizing on their four years of French at Yeading Junior School. It is often the case that the decision to provide children with a particular language is very much dependent upon the resources available to the secondary school at the time. For instance, many of our children were given Spanish rather than French and one could certainly argue the case that this would not be contributing towards building up their vocabulary and conversational skills in French. However, and based on the fact that we wanted to adopt a linguistic approach in our teaching of languages, this issue has become less of a problem, particularly since it has allowed our children simply to transfer their language skills to a different target language. This fact has been clearly shared with the Year 6 children and no one so far has questioned it.

The linguistic approach has allowed children to understand the necessities of learning a language that seems to be foreign to them at the time, and it has given them a better understanding of how languages form, develop and evolve over the years. It also has contributed to their understanding of English or their home language by looking at the common factors that link many of the contemporary world languages.

The story of language learning and acquisition at Yeading Junior School is one of achievements and dreams. It started with a strong vision from the headteacher and the commitment of others to the project; for without the right vision, there can be no accomplishment. However, vision alone is not sufficient unless you also provide funds and resources, commitment to the project, and a dynamic way to deliver the project. All of these factors need to be clearly and consistently modelled if you want these values to be effectively absorbed by each pupil. We wanted all of our pupils to become full participants in their linguistic journey rather than just beneficiaries. They own their linguistic journey.

If the purpose of learning a language is to communicate, then gone are the days when you had to learn a long list of unnecessary vocabulary. Words in isolation serve very little purpose, other than in a testing scenario, which is why all our children learn French, Latin and Spanish within the context of a question, as exemplified earlier in the chapter; for why would you be talking unless they understand the questions and can answer them effectively and without hesitation? For instance, the answers provided will be taken from a range of possible answers. To the simple question *'Comment ça va aujourd'hui?'* ('How are you doing today?'), rather than just responding, as is often the case, with *'Ça va/Ça ne va pas'* ('OK/not OK'), you could get a range of possible answers, such as: *'Ça ne va pas très fort, parce que je ne me sens pas bien – j'ai mal aux dents/ j'ai mal à la tête/ j'ai mal aux jambes'* ('Not great, because I'm not feeling well – I've got toothache/ I've got a headache/my legs are hurting'). However, this requires passion and commitment as well as pride in being able to transfer the language to a different set of questions, which is simply quite remarkable.

In my view, the combination of French and Latin is ideal in a setting like ours as this allows our children to reflect on their own learning and acquisition of the English language. It gives them a greater sense of purpose and contributes towards the development of their sense of identity and belonging. They take pride in their assemblies, in the manipulation of the languages, and in their grammatical understanding. They look forward to their trip abroad and their linguistic exchange. They put themselves forward for organizing French or Latin clubs for the younger ones or for teaching their younger siblings at home.

When it comes to their language awareness and learning, the children certainly embody many of the virtues that are so dear to our school, such as passion, volunteering, curiosity, reflection, dignity and pride. When one class of Year 6 children were asked about which virtue they thought was going to be the most important in their learning and acquisition of a language, a large majority put pride and determination on an equal level, followed by reflection and respect. Although this is only one class, and we need to be aware of the danger in making sweeping generalizations across other classes, it does demonstrate that children not only have a clear understanding of these virtues but they also recognize that in the context of a particular subject they will need to showcase and tap into key features of our school values. For example, one needs determination to study a language as the task itself is certainly not an easy one; they will also take pride in making progress in their language learning and acquisition; and that by doing so, pupils are gaining some understanding of someone else's culture and language, which inevitably leads them to a sense of respect towards other cultures and ways of life.

Yeading Junior School is so richly diverse, both in terms of cultural heritage and linguistic inheritance, that our children are in a way already predisposed to study a variety of languages with passion and devotion. With a wide range of languages already spoken at home, it is therefore essential for any teacher to tap into what's already there, and what then emerges from this jigsaw of diversity is a landscape of multi-lingual unity. Latin, French and Spanish add an additional layer to our global and polyglot community. The delivery of European languages contributes to the enhancement of our international spirit, a spirit of curiosity. This virtue is certainly one our children are exceeding in when it comes to studying languages.

On a final note, it is the headteacher's vision and a love for languages which have helped in transforming and shaping the linguistic landscape at Yeading Junior School. Without a strong interest and the virtues attached to learning a new language, this landscape would be very barren indeed.

References

Bell, B. (2000) *Minimus: Minimus Teacher's Resource Book: Starting Out in Latin*. Cambridge: Cambridge University Press.

Bell, B. (2004) *Minimus: Minimus Secondus Teacher's Resource Book: Moving on in Latin*. Cambridge: Cambridge University Press.

Board, K. and Tinsley, T. (2015) *Language Trends 2014/15. The State of Language Learning in Primary and Secondary Schools in England*. London: British Council and CfBT Education Trust.

Classics for All (2013) *Championing Classics in Schools*. London: King's College. Accessed 25/04/19 at www.classicsforall.org.uk

Department for Education (DfE) (2012) *Making Foreign Languages Compulsory at Key Stage 2*. London: DfE.

Department for Education (DfE) (2013) *Language Programmes of Study: Key Stage 2. National Curriculum in England*. London: DfE.

Department for Education and Skills (DfES) (2002) *Languages for All: Languages for Life – a Strategy for England*. London: DfES.

Chapter 4

Building Networks and Partnerships

CAROLE JONES

Contextual background

This chapter encapsulates the work the school has undertaken with the local community and with wider network partners over a number of years to both inspire children and to effect change in learning and raise attainment. A number of national policies and government papers have been instrumental in influencing our educational journey. In 2001, the notion of schools offering greater all-round experiences was put forward. The governors and I were very keen for the school to be at the forefront of this initiative, known as 'Extended Schools'. Our school continues to promote extended services and very much collaborates with others in an innovative way. We have restructured teams within our school and developed new opportunities for staff, such as our in-house Children and Families team.

The notion of working with the community, within and beyond school, as well as signposting the community to a range of services, has brought significant changes to our practice, most notably in working more closely with parents and wider partners. The Department for Education and Skills (DfES), White Paper *Schools Achieving Success* stated: 'We have a clear picture of a good primary school. It has high expectations of its pupils and delivers high standards in the basics. Its pupils enjoy school and achieve their full potential across a broad and stimulating curriculum' (DfES 2001).

Yeading Junior School embraced the vision of this White Paper and worked hard to ensure that children achieved well and were given every opportunity to be successful, including being offered stimulating opportunities that went beyond the remit of the school and sometimes the school day. These included art projects, drama and sport, as well as exciting reading opportunities linking with the local library. In the White Paper there was recognition that:

> Schools are an important resource for the whole community and close partnerships with other public services can bring great benefits. We will support schools to work with local providers including health and social services, to make available on their site a wide range of easily accessible support for children and their families. Where necessary, the Government will legislate to enable more schools to do this. (DfES 2001)

As supported in the White Paper, Yeading Junior School opened its doors to the community in order to improve opportunities for all children by working even more closely with parents and the wider community, including partner organizations, in order to raise achievement and aspiration. This was an opportune time for the school as this educational driver of change journey was in its infancy, just as I took up my role as headteacher.

LEARNING, WORKING AND ACHIEVING TOGETHER

The above school motto is inclusive of the children, staff, parents, governors and the wider community. We submitted an application in 2004 to become an Extended School hub and leader for a group of schools offering extended services within and beyond the school day. The school was successful in its application. The Extended Schools' agenda enables groups of schools to work together with a range of partners on funded projects aimed to raise the educational attainment of disadvantaged children, offering them support to meet their potential.

The Yeading Cluster collaborative was made up of ten schools initially, including two secondary schools and a special school. The children and staff of these schools have had the opportunity to work together on a number of projects, including interfaith events. The cluster of schools continues to meet and work together on a wide range of different priorities following the end of the formal Extended Schools funded programme. Nine schools remain together currently, with a further school engaging with us more recently.

In 2004, we began a journey of learning that opened up the school as a resource for a rapidly changing community. We realized that the school gate symbolized important cultural differences between many styles of learning that were familiar to parents from wide-ranging cultural backgrounds and the schools' approach to teaching and learning. In November 2004, the Children Act (HMSO 2004) was established and *Every Child Matters* (DfES 2003) brought radical change. At this point the school engaged with the National Pyramid Trust for Children. A great deal of work was undertaken with anti-bullying, and our journey into peer mediation and social action began in earnest.

The Green Paper *Every Child Matters* states:

> The Government wants to integrate education, health and social care services around the needs of children. To achieve this, we want all schools to become extended schools – acting as the hub for services for children, families and other members of the community. Extended schools offer the community and their pupils a range of services (such as childcare, adult learning, health and community facilities) that go beyond their core educational function. (DfES 2003)

It was at this time that the school began to look at the conversion of a disused caretaker's house as a place where parents could meet and share ideas, as well as receive advice and guidance whilst being signposted to other agencies for greater needs. The Green Paper (DfES 2003) goes on to emphasize the importance of considering children's voices when making changes and new provisions, including the consistent theme of consultations with children and young people, as well as the importance of having communities where there is 'somewhere safe to go and something to do'. This not only provides recreational activity for children and young people but also helps to build the fabric of communities and increases young people's skills, confidence and self-esteem. Yeading Junior School places great value on the importance of self-esteem and the involvement of children in their learning. The actions the school took at this stage began to shape the journey of development of the virtuous child that we are currently seeing.

The staff and governors continue to work hard to ensure that there are the very best facilities, resources and teaching programmes available to the children, thus providing every child with a full, varied, balanced and exciting education. The school offers a rich and varied range of extra-curricular activities to support all aspects of learning. The school has a strong belief in the importance of partnerships in terms of raising aspiration, inspiring children and enabling them to reach their potential. Engagement and empowerment are central to our work.

The approach

Our staff come from different cultural backgrounds and many can speak a range of home languages. Cultural traditions are well known and although Yeading Junior School is a community school, a number of faiths are also represented. The first and most important extended activity was to establish a parent/carer group with parent coffee mornings becoming an early feature of this. Initially, to facilitate language development, the groups were cultural; however, opinions quickly changed, and more inclusive and cohesive groups were formed – for example, the popular English for Speakers of Other Languages (ESOL) classes and positive parenting. Views and opinions were sought from parents and a range of activities were established for the benefit of parents and their children.

Transition from one phase of education to another flourished as parents developed greater knowledge and understanding of the curriculum, its application and assessment processes. Parents learned with the children and also learned for their own personal growth and development. This was the advent of a truly cohesive and aspirational community that began to engage fully in the life and vision of the school, embracing its many developments and successes.

At this stage the school began to engage with local organizations and facilities such as the Yeading Library, the Health Promotion team and local police. The school had also begun to reach out to universities to work with social workers in training. Our initial link was with Brunel University London. A professor successfully introduced us to a version of her Families and Schools Together (FAST) programme.

Social work students on placement with the school ran a transition club from Key Stage 1 to Key Stage 2, providing opportunities for families to get together after school, to enjoy spending quality time with their children and to develop relationships with others. This project's aims were to develop social capital. Children and their families were supported by a home/school liaison worker and a learning mentor. As time moved on, and the impact of these roles on the children and parents was seen to be extremely effective, another learning mentor was recruited together with, more recently, a school social worker.

Links within and beyond the school community

Wide-ranging links, both locally and nationally, with many partners for the benefit of the pupils and wider community have always been, and remain, a feature of the school. Our early work has been featured in case studies published by the Training and Development Agency for Schools (TDA 2009) responsible for the in-service training of teachers and other educational staff (now known as the Department for Education), and the Centre for Social Justice. This case study outlines our work in the community and the impact it has on children and their parents.

Initial community links included Healthy Hillingdon and their partners. The school was represented on the steering group for this local authority health-promoting team, and our co-chair of governors was formally the manager. We have undertaken many health-related projects, including playground friends and a peer-mediator programme. A group of peer-mediator children attended Number 11 Downing Street to be awarded Diana Awards for their work in social action, which involved running friendship clubs for their peers.

The greatest source of community links is associated with our Community House, which offers a safe space where the community shares in wide-ranging projects. Many services are available for parents/carers, including ESOL, counselling and coffee mornings. Links with a variety of agencies initially included the Safer Neighbourhood Team. Projects that were run included the Women's Role Model project linked to the Victoria and Albert Museum (V&A). Mothers created tablecloths portraying their respective lives and cultural stories. Their children congratulated them publicly by presenting them with certificates, thus engendering pride, parent to child, and instilling respect, one to the other.

The school has undertaken a considerable amount of work in response to its duty to promote community cohesion (Department for Communities and Local Government [DCLG] 2006). In 2009, I was appointed as a national community cohesion advocate with the National College of School Leadership (NCSL). This was a project that I had been selected to work on with other advocates, leading the way on improving community cohesion outcomes through schools.

An example of cohesive work was the National Heartstone project, 'Festival of Flight', which had been delivered in Hillingdon in 2009 and was rebranded, at the time, as 'Reach for the Sky', a project that focused on helping young people to understand discrimination and build aspiration. The project had been a joint endeavour between Brunel University London,

Healthy Hillingdon and Yeading Junior School as part of the then Hillingdon Stronger Communities partnership; it was subsequently cascaded to other schools, with the young people who had already participated in the project acting as mentors. The school put together a booklet entitled *Joining the Pieces,* which summarized some best-practice models of working that had been developed with Yeading Junior School and other partners.

As mentioned above, the TDA had been particularly interested in the work that had been undertaken at Yeading Community House, which opened officially in February 2008. The case study stated the following:

> Yeading Cluster Schools House was formerly a caretaker's residence, which has been converted into a 'safe space 'for parents; the house was conceived as a way of addressing the isolation and loneliness experienced by many parents from diverse ethnic backgrounds; it offers a wide range of activities, with regular sessions on health matters, weekly drop-in counselling sessions, a parenting programme and a family support worker, education welfare officer and police liaison officer. (TDA 2009)

The case study captured the success of the Community House, which continues to be such an important feature of the school. The outcomes outlined below referred to both parents and children, and it is through this joint work that we have enabled parents to have greater aspirations for their children and for the children themselves to become more articulate and skillful learners.

- There is a high level of parental engagement at weekly assemblies and school activities.
- More than 1,000 visits have been made to take part in activities at the house.
- Children's and parents' self-confidence is 'phenomenal'.
- The ESOL programme has resulted in some parents securing employment as a result of their improving English skills.
- Children's average point scores have increased.
- Enhanced community engagement and cohesion is helping to break down cross-cultural barriers.
- Pupil and staff motivation is high.
- The partnership between the school, parents and children is highly evolved and a high level of trust has been built.

- Four peer mediators have won a national award that will soon be presented to them at Downing Street.

The school noted that a celebratory event involving approximately 150 women would be held at the school on 19 June 2010.

The curriculum

At an early stage a corporate identity was established for the collaboration of schools. The Conservative–Liberal Democrat coalition government (DfE 2010) referred to broadening the curriculum and providing greater opportunities for children, leading to more holistic learning experiences and resulting in improved attainment and life. The school continues to provide an exciting and innovative curriculum.

Character education is now at the heart of the school and threads through every aspect of the curriculum and learning. Prior to undertaking the journey in character education and the establishment of a set of core virtues, we worked hard to engage families in order to improve the self-esteem and confidence of learners. The partnership and engagement of families supported by services provided a landscape whereby children could flourish and learn well, whilst also understanding the impact they can have on society through their actions. The excellent role modelling of basic values had commenced. From an early stage the school worked on interfaith projects, which were particularly important in our diverse community. Positive feedback from the children at an early interfaith event indicated how important this was:

A great opportunity to meet others from different cultures.

I strongly recommend the event continues. It is helpful to the community.

Our original strategies have been most successful in developing wide-ranging links with local partners for the benefit of the children, families, cluster schools and the local community. The school community has developed the skills to self-evaluate and recognize where to aspire to next. We have learned a great deal about building on the strength of the community and involving key people at the start of the journey. We have also learned about the importance of auditing the needs and views of the community well, in order to strengthen and inspire all its members. Through developing effective partnerships with a wider range of organizations (see Chapter 8), we have been able to add breadth to the curriculum, which has led to greater challenges for learners.

Through working in an effective partnership with other schools in our locality, we have been able to enhance curriculum development. Schools have been able to undertake writing projects and moderation together, work on projects that have enhanced children's understanding of social action and develop staff professional development. A community choir was established and a regular dance festival takes place. Children from the cluster schools have discussed issues together and taken part in charitable campaigns, and some have engaged in activities to raise self-esteem. Religious Education (RE) coordinators from the collaborative schools and elsewhere in the local authority have worked more closely together on activities as a result of strengthened school collaborations.

Schools working collaboratively in this way, particularly where they have evolved from an extended services remit, reflect the design of the Schools White Paper *The Importance of Teaching*, which states:

> Good schools play a vital role as promoters of health and wellbeing in the local community and have always had good pastoral systems. They understand well the connections between pupils' physical and mental health, their safety, and their educational achievement. They create an ethos focused on achievement for all, where additional support is offered early to those who need it, and where the right connections are made to health, social care and other professionals who can help pupils overcome whatever barriers to learning are in their way. Good schools work with parents, community organizations and local agencies to create a healthy, safe and respectful environment in school, after school, and on the way to and from school. Good teachers instil an ethos where aspiration is the best reason for children to avoid harmful behaviour. (DfE 2010)

Legacy of Extended Schools

The original Extended Schools programme has led to enhanced communication between schools in the locality, including a continuing sharing of expertise. As a group of schools, we are able to trial different services or access them together, such as early intervention services for raising pupils' self-esteem. We have also been able to access sources of funding together to develop activities (e.g. an annual event at the Beck Theatre, which is organized by the Yeading Cluster and called 'Together We Can Make a Change'). Through dance and drama, children have been able to share values and demonstrate how they have made an impact on their locality. Through shared services, we are able to make a difference. Yeading Junior School continues to offer life-long learning opportunities for parents, many of whom have gained National Vocational Qualifications (NVQs) on our school site. Others have been able to gain in confidence so that they can go back into the workplace.

The student social work unit in the Community House in conjunction with new Buckinghamshire University and the London Borough of Hillingdon, was officially launched on 7 February 2008. Social work students continue on placement with the school some ten years later. They act as key workers for children, support our internal Children and Families team and take a full and active role in all aspects of safeguarding. The students have become excellent role models as learners for the children. In turn, the children are keen to learn more about university and how they too could aspire to go there one day. The students enable children to conduct clubs and activities for their peers by supporting them and becoming the adult in attendance.

In the first three months of the establishment of the Community House, 220 people attended the house to either liaise with the agencies engaged or to take part in other support networks, including coffee mornings or training. Numbers attending are no longer gathered in this way; what the school is more interested in now is the parental understanding of children's learning, the impact of those who attend curriculum-related workshops, and also the parents' understanding of character education and its impact on the children and themselves as families. A good partnership has been established and continued with the Hillingdon Adult Education Service, which currently offers learning opportunities to a number of parents. This, in turn, benefits the children.

Enhanced sports provision has taken place in the school as a result of increased partnership work. Children have become more resilient and determined in respect of sporting activities. Currently, a number of children have a weekly opportunity to run on the Brunel University running track in the footsteps of Olympians. Children have also been signposted to local clubs (e.g. Hayes Cricket Club). There has also been increased involvement with the secondary schools sector.

Developing partnerships and networks has become a real strength of the school. The children have learned a great deal through observing partnership work, and they are influenced by this when working together. It is not uncommon in school for children to seek to set up activities to support others during their own time, breaktime or lunchtime. Such activities have involved children forming a small group, developing a plan and delivering support to their peers. An example of this would be a group that supports newly arrived children from overseas with reading at lunchtime. Another example was the Arts and Crafts club for younger children that was set up by the older 'Special Agents' after school, in order to raise funds to support a club run by young girls in Ecuador.

Clearly the journey has developed and evolved over time. The school continues to hold the Tribal Extended Services Quality Mark (an interim assessment successfully took place in 2017). Tribal Extended Services (March 2019) state: 'The Quality Mark aims to undertake effective self-evaluation and continuous improvement for English and Mathematics, which drives better outcomes for pupils, their families and society.' This is an important accolade for the school and ensures that we regularly evaluate our own progress in partnership working and have this externally assessed. We also received the 10 Year Basic Skills Quality Mark in 2019 which is awarded to schools that provide excellence in Mathematics and English and have maintained this over a ten-year period.

The school now links with a number of national charities and organizations, including the WE Schools, Team London and #iwill. Through these associations, children have honed their character virtues. A current project that links with the DePaul Trust for the homeless has enabled children to bring in items to provide a significant number of items to make up survival kits for the homeless. Links with the local Salvation Army and their work with the homeless have further extended our reach and efforts to support them. Staff have also committed their support at the Salvation Army soup kitchen. The school has a very strong partnership with the Northwood Live at Home Scheme (which features in Chapter 5 in relation to intergenerational learning).

Through these partnerships, children are learning to show dignity, respect and compassion. They have also learned much about teamwork, determination and resilience. The intergenerational work, in particular, has been enhanced by the numbers of children who are growing up in extended families, and they are both learning skills and utilizing skills to support their volunteering.

Another close partnership that has built up over time has been with the Yeading Library. Children and their families have engaged in reading activities, performed drama pieces and sung at Christmas events. Reading circles have been established for both children and parents. Parents who are relatively new to English have been coached in reading the same story book as their children back in school in order to ascertain whether this leads to greater engagement by the children and whether parents are better able to support more challenging comprehension questions with their children. The school has also joined in themed events and special occasions.

As mentioned earlier, each year the school hires the Beck Theatre in Hayes on behalf of the cluster schools, which is still funded through an educational initiative bid associated with Extended Schools. An annual event entitled 'Together We Can Make a Change' takes place in front of a packed audience of parents, relatives and community members. Each school takes to the stage with a group of pupils to present highlights of their social action through prose, drama, song and music. The event teaches us much about the pride the children and families have in their local community. It is an occasion where skills and talents are at the fore and there is an abundance of great respect. The final task for the schools is the joint singing of a selected song known to all, which is quite a moving finale. A member of the WE Schools team wrote the following after being invited to make a presentation about social action at the 2016 event:

> I feel really privileged to be working alongside Yeading Junior School. It is truly inspiring to see such dedicated staff that are passionate about building character and increasing academic attainment through building resilience and creativity. It is also the pupils and families that made yesterday so special. The Yeading Cluster is not the sort of cluster I see every day. It is so unique to see such a diverse range of pupils and parents come together to celebrate and acknowledge the power of working together. There was so much talent in the Beck Theatre last night. It really does show what is possible when you aim high. Thank you so much for being part of WE Schools. (Personal communication)

What do our virtuous children at Yeading Junior School know about building partnerships and networks? They are fortunate to have enjoyed so many rich experiences, which are reflected upon and talked about throughout their years of schooling. Opportunities such as speaking in prestigious venues and meeting athletes, company directors, university graduates and other professionals have all brought them value and aspiration for the future.

The children have come to understand the processes involved in engagement and in developing partnerships. For example, they understood that having attended an Annual General Meeting (AGM) at the Northwood Live at Home Scheme and meeting Professor Heinz Wolff, that he would one day be able to share his thoughts and ideas on social capital in their school hall. What an amazing experience for those young learners who learned all about his passion for science, associated university work, television appearances and his concern about others through his 'Give and Take Care' venture. Professor Wolff related well to the school's virtues and was extremely delighted that curiosity was one of these. He told the children that they should always be curious learners. He sat amongst them and showed real joy at the children's responses to his challenging questions. The visit from (the now late) Professor Heinz Wolff is one that will always be remembered and treasured. We often reflect on his pleasure at curiosity being a Yeading Junior School virtue. The children clearly understood that being curious had led him to undertake great things.

Leaders, at all levels, have a significant role in terms of supporting children to understand the importance of *doing good*. Leaders, moreover, enable children to learn and experience the impact of doing good, both on themselves and on others. In order to create an ethos where children flourish in this way, there needs to be a clear vision and intent that is shared by all members of the team and community. Whether it has been partnerships set up by me as headteacher, or by teachers or para-professionals in the school, it has been important for everyone to know about them and to understand how these partnerships can have a profound effect on learning and aspiration. Partnerships have also become an asset to the school since they can often provide valuable learning resources and opportunities, as well as funding that can create further exciting opportunities. The children at Yeading Junior School have certainly become adept themselves at suggesting links when they have taken part in activities or represented the school.

The WE movement, formerly known as 'Free the Children', continues to provide a platform for our social action. It was brought to Yeading Junior School in 2013 through an invitation sent out to schools by Team London.[1] As a school where social action had already assumed a central

---

1   Team London is the Mayor of London's volunteering and social action team.

role, we were appropriately poised to take part in this to further enrich our curriculum and develop our projects. For some primary schools this may have been a little early in terms of their involvement in social action.

An engaging assembly was delivered by an inspirational ambassador from Team London. The children were particularly impressed with the video clip of a WE Day celebration held in Toronto, Canada. It appeared at the time that all of the children were anxious to attend the inaugural event at the Wembley Arena in London. However, it soon became apparent to the children that each school would only be allocated a few tickets and that you could not buy them, they had to be earned through work that would bring change to others. Children reflected on this concept and set to work collating their actions and embedding them in letters, putting forward their own case for attending the event. These letters are still sent to me on an annual basis, and one such letter, received from a Year 5 child, reads:

> I would be extremely happy if you accepted this letter, so I could get a ticket to WE Day. I, myself, am very fond of charity work, and as of my interest I have really put all of my effort into this. WE Day is an exciting experience for me, therefore I would really appreciate it if you gave me a ticket to this AMAZING once in a lifetime experience. I like doing charity work, mainly because it's for those people in need of support, and my contribution to every charity, like everyone else, really makes a difference.

Our relationship with the WE organization has sustained and flourished over time. It is something to really celebrate. The far-reaching impact of this relationship, in terms of the children, the community and links with others, makes it an interesting case study and one that shines a light on the importance of forging strong, sustainable relationships where the voice of the school can also be heard and used.

This link is a fine example of where leadership has expertly driven the programme forward, identifying it as a clear platform for addressing local and global social actions. The school takes part in the organization's year-long programme of action. The children are well aware of the five pillars of impact associated with WE: Education, Water, Health, Food and Opportunity. On their website, the organization outlines the objective of each pillar and its impact. Furthermore, there are teaching suggestions and resources for schools to enable them to devise action plans within the curriculum to enhance children's learning and understanding about making a difference in the world. One member of staff said: 'These resources are helpful in planning social action. They create a clearer picture on how we can successfully embed social action into irresistible lessons.' Over time, other members of staff have echoed the same sentiment. The learning framework and associated resources featured within Figure 4.1 have provided invaluable guidance and insights into the programme. These can be adapted accordingly to suit the needs of the school.

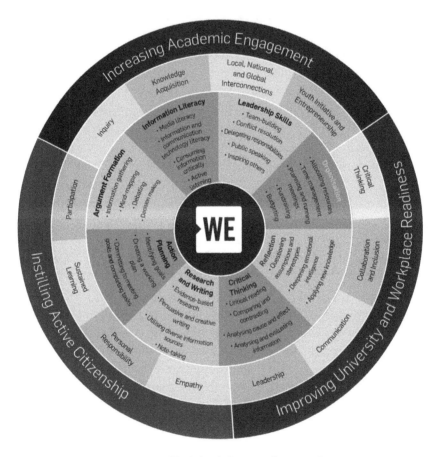

Figure 4.1 WE Schools learning framework

As time has moved on, the school has liaised even more closely with WE UK. We were delighted in 2015 when one of our children stood on the WE Day stage and shared her social action activities within school with at least 12,000 young people. In preparation for this we worked with the team member in charge of speakers and also engaged in a range of other preparatory activities. Meanwhile, her peers back in school, as well as the group of children attending the Wembley Arena engaged in the whole event. Those back in school tuned in to the day's activities on the whiteboard in the classroom through a web link on the school's IT system. This brought great excitement to the school, and others expressed a desire to emulate her role.

Five of our Special Agents had an incredible opportunity at WE Day UK on 7 March 2019, when they appeared on stage in front of thousands of young people, retelling Iqbal Masih's story. This story is central to the origin of the WE movement and is why it was set up by Marc and Craig Keilberger. Iqbal Masih was a child labourer who spoke out against his captors, was shot for doing so, and died. This story, when read by Craig Keilberger in a newspaper in Canada, had such an impact on him and his brother that they worked together with school friends to make a difference and have subsequently devoted their lives to the movement. It is the essence of this story and the ages of those concerned that had such a profound impact on our young learners, particularly our children in Years 5 and 6.

Therefore, it was really poignant and such an honour that the children were invited to retell this story on stage. They did so with compassion, respect and the determination to themselves make a difference. Their courage and the strength of their performance, which was broadcast by *Cable News Network* (*CNN*) on behalf of WE Schools, had all the hallmarks of our virtues. The children demonstrated empathy, and through their experience they became more intuitive in discussions held in school and on the media about freedom. These children were interviewed by *CNN* whilst attending WE Day and their articulate comments were broadcast on television. They stated the following:

Freedom for me means having the right to do whatever you want to do that benefits you whenever you want.

My Freedom Day is a way to speak up for others who may not have a voice. It's a way to connect with other people who don't have the rights to be heard. Our campaigns want people to be free to be able to make their own decisions.

This whole opportunity was not a chance happening but a testament to all of the work the school had taken part in over a number of years and which has attracted attention both nationally and internationally. Our efforts had reached the very core of the organization in Canada from where we were chosen to engage in this way.

Being an active part of WE Day was not the only experience the children had to have their voices heard widely. March 14 in 2019 was an exciting and extraordinary day of learning for everyone at Yeading Junior School. Leaders from the WE organization and a team from *CNN*, together with an award-winning correspondent, visited the school to broadcast a news item on #MyFreedomDay. #MyFreedomDay is an annual, 24-hour, pupil-driven day, where CNN broadcasts live from school locations across the world, showcasing how young people speak up and take action about modern-day slavery and share thoughts on what freedom means to them. Yeading Junior School was selected to be the one school in the UK to present their thoughts to the world.

The school had already taken part earlier in a 'WE Are Silent' event, one of WE Schools' campaigns, raising awareness of those young people who do not have a voice and are struggling to have their basic human rights such as education. The school led an event across a cluster of schools whereby the whole group converged on a neighbouring university by walking and using transport to take part in a range of workshop activities led by each school. The sponsor money raised was given to the education pillar at WE for further development of schools globally, so that all children have the opportunity to learn. It is through involvement in activities like these that the children begin to understand global issues such as poverty and how their work can enable others to become empowered and not exploited. Our children are indeed recognized as 'Keepers of the World', an expression that was coined by one of our regular visitors to the school and which has since become part of the school's lexicon.

On 14 March 2019, the school wholly embraced work around freedom. Our special Agents of Change took part in a workshop led by expert WE facilitators. Through taking part in hands-on activities, they learned to discuss and share root causes of modern-day slavery and explored the tools to make a difference. They also found out about how education empowers people and makes a significant difference to their lives. The children ably and articulately answered questions on live television, sharing their opinions with the world. Some children were given brief scenarios to look at and were asked to share their thoughts and opinions. The response to one of the scenarios exemplified just how profoundly they were thinking about others. They very much rose to this challenging situation and reflected on the knowledge. Their singing of an inspirational song drew them together in unity and was heard across the world. The children found it poignant when a message from the songwriter was shared with them. These are the moments that enable children to further understand mutual respect, compassion and the impact they have on others. Parents were delighted that their children were engaged in positive action. In fact, families had already engaged with their children in creating models, posters and pictures to explain what freedom meant to them. Not only does engagement in this way continue to consolidate a greater understanding of the importance of the virtues threaded through school life and learning it also has an impact on the children's skills, as shown in this piece of writing from a Special Agent pupil in Year 6, inspired by our special day:

> Before the event took place, the Special Agents of Change were all invited to a workshop to get a taster of the day. We each had a different profile and instantly put ourselves in their shoes. I couldn't believe what I was reading. Thinking about how much of a struggle their lives were, made me quiver anxiously. We all realized how fortunate we were to be able to have a voice and speak out for causes we believe in. I was shocked as to what people had been through in life and how we may sometimes take things for granted when some people may live in appalling conditions.

The school acknowledges the effectiveness of working with large organizations such as WE and embedding their programme within the school's eclectic mix of programmes and activities that form part of our social action platform. The children enjoy planning and setting up partnerships within school in order to support wide-ranging activities for others, both at school and beyond. Following our recent 'WE Are Silent' walk, I received the following accolade for the children from one of our partner organizations, which wrote the following: 'I chatted the whole way home about the morning, and the self-esteem and the confidence of each and every one of the children reflects upon the amazing all-round education they receive at Yeading Junior School.'

The joy and enthusiasm we gain from working in this way has a really positive impact on our children's learning and well-being.

References

Department for Communities and Local Government (DCLG) (2006) *Strong and Prosperous Communities.* The Local Government White Paper. London: DCLG.

Department for Education (DfE) (2010) *The Importance of Teaching.* White Paper. London: DfE.

Department for Education and Skills (DfES) (2001) *Schools Achieving Success*. White Paper. London: DfES.

Department for Education and Skills (DfES) (2003) *Every Child Matters*. Green Paper. London: DfES.

Families and Schools Together (FAST) (2017) *Early Intervention Foundation Guidebook*. London: EIF. Accessed 25/04/19 at https://guidebook.eif.org.uk/programmes/families-and-schools-together

Training and Development Agency for Schools (TDA) (2009) *Transforming Lives: Special Schools and Extended Services*. London: TDA.

Tribal Extended Services (2019) 'Quality Mark Primary.' Accessed 25/04/10 at https://info.tribalgroup.com/quality-mark-for-primary-schools

UK Legislation (2004) *Children Act*. London: HMSO.

Chapter 5

Multi-Generational Work

ANGELA FLUX

This chapter illustrates how multi-generational learning opportunities can support character education in children and stimulate social contact for older people. Both are important social challenges today. The work has been piloted by a partnership between the Methodist Homes for the Aged (MHA) Northwood Live at Home Scheme and Yeading Junior School. The 200 people membership of the Live at Home Scheme spans several generations, especially when one includes the further cohort of 70 volunteers who tend to be active retired people. For this reason, I have used the term 'multi-generational', although 'intergenerational' is often used within an educational context. The Beth Johnson Foundation describes intergenerational practice as follows:

> Intergenerational practice aims to bring people together in purposeful, mutually beneficial activities which promote greater understanding and respect between generations and contributes to building more cohesive communities. Intergenerational practice is inclusive, building on the positive resources that the young and old have to offer each other and those around them. (Beth Johnson Foundation 2011)

A programme of interventions was co-designed to explore how multi-generational learning opportunities can increase social contact, improving the emotional health of all those involved. The effect of loneliness and isolation on mortality is comparable to the impact of well-known risk factors such as obesity and cigarette smoking (Holt-Lundstad *et al.* 2015). This raises the question: Could social contact across generations improve lives, adding years to life and life to years?

The Guide to Intergenerational Practice (Beth Johnson Foundation, 2011) uses a scale to describe types of intervention and levels of interaction which span the continuum from low (1) to high level (7). Interventions described in this chapter are in the upper range of this scale, being offered weekly during term time for a period of 6–7 weeks. This contact level allows time for relationships to form between participants rather than being one-off encounters. The programme of partnership work between the MHA Northwood Live at Home and Yeading Junior School has sought to reinforce the school character virtues, particularly team work, respect, resilience, dignity, compassion, reflection and determination. Groups of between six to eight Year 5 children come off-site to meet older people from an area about ten miles away from their school. Groups attended weekly for a term at a time, over a three-year period.

This partnership programme supported children's ability to relate beyond their peer group in a setting with people considerably older than themselves and not in a teacher–student relationship. Whilst school children have opportunities to relate to parents, carers, teachers, siblings and peer groups, opportunities with older people in the community can often be more limited. Likewise, older people may have limited contact with much younger people in today's increasingly segmented society, especially if they have no children or their children have moved away.

Our three-year programme of interventions influenced the school ethos by providing a regular volunteering opportunity with older people. This was due to the number of children who participated and reported back to their peers. Parental permission was sought, and no parents objected to the children being involved in the programme, so the programme to enhance character education through contact across generations was developed in partnership with the parents. On some occasions, parents came to events to see their children interacting and performing to multiple generations of people; parents and staff demonstrated active interest and support. Weekly iPad training sessions evolved into times of mutual learning and sharing skills, experiences and interests. Children were given a choice as to what they did and who they interacted with. Children were given the opportunity to volunteer and were then selected by staff. Those children who needed to further develop confidence or interpersonal skills such as empathy or communication were given priority in the selection process.

Societal deficits and need –
why we planned what we did

In the UK in the 21st century, we face interesting challenges regarding how many opportunities there are for children and young people to relate to older people, as the Intergenerational Foundation reports:

> Children now have a mere 5.5% chance of having someone aged over 65 living in their area compared to a 15% chance in 1991, while the level of segregation between retirees and young adults has roughly doubled in the same period. (Intergenerational Foundation 2016)

Factors relating to this change include greater social mobility, immigration, economic pressures on parents to be in paid employment, greater variety and more frequent change in what constitutes a person's family, and people being required to move for better jobs or to find affordable housing. This can mean that established communities have been disrupted. In some cultures, it is not uncommon for children to have lost contact with grandparents, whereas in some cases grandparents may live in the family home. Adults may be unable to care for ageing parents in ways that would have been the norm in previous generations. Visiting family may occur less commonly, competing with other domestic and leisure alternatives. Conversely, intergenerational contact may increase in some circumstances as grandparents are called upon to provide childminding while parents work.

With such factors at play, Kingman (2016) reports that in England and Wales we are seeing an increase in the segmentation of society and that many children and young people have limited exposure to learning from their elders. In some larger university cities, the gap between young people and the older generation is becoming increasingly evident, with lack of consideration and understanding happening in both directions. Regenerated city centres are increasingly the preserve of the under-30s, while middle-aged people dominate coastal areas. Data analysis (Kingman 2016) indicates levels of generational segregation in different cities, with Cardiff identified as the most segregated.

Alongside this lack of intergenerational contact, children frequently have limited opportunities to play in an unsupervised way through which they can assess and take risks (Voce 2008). This limits their learning from experience and from their peers. Adults in their lives – parents and carers, teachers and those in the medical profession – are increasingly aware of the need to protect and safeguard children, especially as the media profiles cases of abduction, paedophilia, gang violence and radicalization. This has led to a risk-averse culture that finds expression in overbearing health and safety policies which fail to weigh benefits of a given activity against the risks involved. Whether it is elderly care providers or those caring for children and young people, we tend to err on the side of caution for fear of litigation, depriving individuals of opportunities which could significantly improve their physical, social and emotional wellbeing.

Research from the University of Birmingham (Arthur *et al.* 2015) found that when asked what single change they would make to achieve better character education, teachers recommended that schools should provide more 'free space' where students could be themselves and do things they really like without having to think about exam scores. This research confirmed that there is concern for the education and development of a child's whole character, which is central to good practice, yet 80 per cent of teachers thought the UK's assessment system hinders this. This finding influenced how we adjusted our multi-generational sessions and allowed children to volunteer to come, select the activity of their choice and choose who they spend time with. Young people's identity is in part formed by their sense of place and the social relationships they have to develop essential life skills. Research from the Office for National Statistics (ONS 2018a) found that feeling safe walking in one's area after dark, liking one's neighbourhood and feeling a sense of belonging are specifically associated with greater wellbeing.

In January 2018, the Social Care Institute for Excellence (SCIE) looked at how commissioners can commission to tackle loneliness and social isolation, and the micro-commissioning of smaller, more local organizations is being encouraged to address this aspect of mental and emotional health in an ageing population (Holmes and Thompson 2018). Self-reported loneliness and depression are increasing, in both young and older people, with frequent media coverage of the need for increased investment in preventative measures and care provision. The evidence base for interventions that work to address these issues is emerging but is not conclusive, especially since 'loneliness and social isolation are conditions difficult to identify, complex to address and hard to resolve' (Holmes and Thompson 2018). Evidence that social connectivity is key to promoting emotional and mental health, which does impact physical health, resulted in some interest for general practitioners (GPs) to prescribe social activities rather than anti-depressants.

The Office for National Statistics (ONS 2018b) recognizes the importance of developing national indicators of loneliness across all age groups and measuring this. Based upon the need and evidence outlined above and associated challenges, we introduced a micro-intervention to bring our communities together and explore the benefits of multi-generational social contact.

Yeading Junior School initiatives

Over the last 20 years Yeading Junior School has developed an exceptional programme focused on promoting the emotional health and wellbeing of children and giving them skills for life. This has taken a range of forms including Healthy Schools, Pyramid Clubs, the Families and School Together (FAST) programme, peer support friendship groups to reduce incidents of bullying, mentor support by social work students, parental engagement and the promotion of volunteering linked to the WE Day initiative.[1]

Children are encouraged to participate, reflect on their emotional health and work with their own feelings and those of others. Opportunities to learn outside the classroom have been valued and celebrated within the whole school community. Parents have engaged in community projects aimed at realizing and recognizing their culture and identity. An example of this was when parents worked with groups of people from their own cultural backgrounds to create tablecloths which had artistic depictions of what values were important to them. They presented their artwork to their children and school staff. Children saw their parents being affirmed within the school community and participating in the life of the school. By identifying what parents value and celebrating diversity within the school community, we have worked towards common values and active respect, enabling parents to be partners in the education of their children. Some trips were organized to encourage parents and children to learn together off-site; for example, we took a group of children and parents to RAF Northolt. This was part of the Healthy Hillingdon Project, 'Festival of Flight',

---

1   This history is more fully explained in Flux (2013) 'Health Promotion – Connecting People and Place.' In C. Davies, R. Flux, M. Hales and J. Walmsley (eds) *Better Health in Harder Times: Active Citizens and Innovation on the Frontline.* Bristol: Policy Press.

when children were encouraged to think about overcoming barriers: geographical, physical and emotional.

Children and parents have been encouraged to offer peer support to others with a view to reducing racial and cultural tensions, promoting a climate of acceptance, learning and celebration. The Community House, an innovation I instigated with the governing body and the London Borough of Hillingdon many years ago, has been a focus for this active parental engagement and signals a commitment to include the wider community into the life of the school, whilst maintaining safety for all. It is a place where parents can learn more about the society in which they live, as well as learn to relate to and support parents who may be struggling. Parents are developing a greater understanding of school life and participating in the school, and some are gaining skills to enhance their employability or parenting potential. Research shows that neighbourhoods have an impact on outcomes for child and adolescent wellbeing (Leventhal and Brooks-Gunn 2000). Yeading Junior School and the MHA Northwood Live at Home Scheme value community assets, people and places and operate an asset-based approach to building safer and stronger communities.

Character education is about building a foundation for life-long learning; supporting successful relationships at home, in the community and workplace; and developing personal values and virtues for sustainable participation in a globalized world. Multi-generational programmes provide an opportunity for much of this learning, and leisure and faith groups within the community enable some of these to occur. By meeting people who are significantly older, children and young people can see how others have lived full and rewarding lives and continue to do so. They can also develop empathy as older people recount how they have overcome challenges or difficult circumstances. There will be people from various age groups coping with disability or other challenges. Sharing in learning and social events brings opportunities for increased sensitivity and appreciation of what is experienced together. By learning, contributing to communities and maintaining social relationships, younger and older people can offer stimulation and insight to each other.

Northwood Live at Home Scheme

Where people, young or old, find a social group which offers friendship and support, this enhances their perception of wellbeing. The mission statement of the MHA charity is *bringing quality to later life*. For some, this will translate into more pleasure, a sense of purpose, independence and dignity. There is no single, coherent measure covering wellbeing for older people, nor is there agreement as to when later life starts. Feeling useful and volunteering by giving to others has been shown to improve positive mental health outcomes, especially for older people (Van Willigen 2000).

In this scheme, member participants are aged over 60 and deemed eligible to be beneficiaries of the charity. All have had an assessment, during which their perception of emotional or mental health was gathered. This is used as a baseline from which to measure any changes. There are, however, many variables that increase our sense of happiness or wellbeing, which means the sole effect of the Northwood Live at Home Scheme activities should be interpreted with some caution.

Age UK and the University of Southampton (Green *et al.* 2017) developed an Index of Wellbeing in Later Life, which shows that engagement in creative and cultural activities makes the highest contribution of 5.75 per cent to overall wellbeing. Having a longstanding illness or disability has a negative effect of 4.21 per cent. Additional findings report:

> Social and civic participation and creative and cultural participation are all important, together making up almost ⅛ of total wellbeing in later life. This suggests that active engagement with the world around you is hugely important to us all, whether you go to the opera or participate in a community group. (Green *et al.* 2017, p.7)

This research indicates that for those aged over 60+ the average wellbeing fell short by 47 per cent for a high proportion of older people in the UK.

The Office for National Statistics (ONS 2018b) is currently developing national indicators of loneliness. The government launched its first loneliness strategy and recognizes that it is a serious public health issue which has significant costs in terms of physical ill-health that can emerge from people feeling depressed, anxious and socially disconnected (Marsh 2018). GPs are encouraged to prescribe social activities such as dance classes, cookery and leisure pursuits which enable communities to reconnect.

With members participating in the Live at Home Scheme, we gather data concerning how they perceive their mental wellbeing, using the statements, questions and response options shown in Table 5.1.

Table 5.1 Questions used to capture perceptions of mental wellbeing

On a scale of 1 (low) to 5 (high), please respond to the following statements:
I've been feeling optimistic about the future. I've been feeling useful. I've been feeling relaxed. I've been dealing with problems well. I've been thinking clearly. I've been feeling close to other people. I've been able to make up my mind about things.
How often do you feel lonely?
Hardly ever Never Some of the time Often
How often do you have a meaningful conversation with a friend, family or neighbour?
Most days Once or twice a week Once or twice a month Less than once a month Never
How often do you have company and social contact?
Most days Once or twice a week Once or twice a month Less than once a month Never

We then offer a social programme, with something for them to participate in each weekday. Volunteer drivers assist with transport, and if people are unable to come to any activities, we organize a 'befriender' to visit them. Activities include seated exercises, yoga, trips, lunches, singing sessions and regular friendship groups involving arts and crafts, quizzes and lunch. Previously, activities had exclusively been a service for older people, but the approach described here shifts the model towards co-designed engagement using local resources of schools and colleges.

As a result of pilot work, multi-generational opportunities have been extended more widely for those who want to meet with children and young people. Children and young people are invited to one or two of the regular sessions on offer each week.

Multi-generational partnership

Our multi-generational programme spans cultures, religious and faith perspectives, age ranges and socio-economic differences. Yeading Junior School is located within the southern part of the London Borough of Hillingdon. The MHA Northwood Live at Home Scheme was started in 1997 by Churches Together in Northwood, situated within the northern part of the London Borough of Hillingdon. When the multi-generational programme started, members were predominantly white British females, a majority of whom were in their eighties and nineties.

Children attending our initial pilot were in Year 5, volunteers were middle-aged and recently retired adults from the Northwood area, and most members of the scheme have some form of age-related illness or disability. The scheme offers physical activities appropriate to the age and stage of each member and encourages activities that promote social interaction, cognitive functioning and participation.

Both the scheme and the school are organizations committed to an inclusive approach receptive towards those of all faiths and those of none. This partnership builds upon my working relationship with the headteacher. I was previously Head of Health Promotion in Public Health in NHS Hillingdon. I have been on the governing body prior to this headteacher's appointment and am currently co-chair as well as scheme manager for the MHA Northwood Live at Home Scheme. The school had worked with the Health Promotion team to pilot initiatives that would increase the children's mental health, the parents' aspirations and a sense of belonging. The focus had predominantly been on children and the immediate school community. This relationship laid the foundation for a multi-generational initiative which spanned the borough and crossed generations. This contextual background information illuminates the importance of relationship-building between key leaders in organizations to *plan, execute, review* and *evaluate* collaborative learning. The National Audit Office recognizes the importance of partnership relationships as fundamental to the success of Local Authorities:

> Providing local public services, which offer value for money and are tailored to the needs of different communities is an immensely complex task. It requires central and local government to work closely together and to make best use of a wide range of other agencies. (National Audit Office 2006, p.1)

Particular emphasis was placed on the importance of clarity of purpose and well-defined responsibilities. In our work together, our purpose was to increase social engagement across generations in such a way that enhanced everyone's sense of wellbeing: children, young people, volunteers and our members. We respected the roles of staff and clarified who would cover various aspects such as risk assessments, researching the evidence base on reducing loneliness, training for staff involved (e.g. safeguarding, first aid), venue hire or transport arrangements, parental consent, provision of resources, monitoring and feedback.

Launch event

We launched the partnership and multi-generational development to all key stakeholders, such as the MHA Northwood Live at Home Scheme (local support group and members) and representatives from the Yeading Junior School community, at a public event, notably, the 2015 Annual General Meeting (AGM). We invited the late Professor Heinz Wolff, someone who had modelled life-long learning and who would not only be known by the older people but would also be inspirational to the children. Professor Wolff was well remembered for *The Great Egg Race* television programme on BBC 2, broadcast between 1979 and 1986. He was a renowned scientist, pioneer of bioengineering, inventor and social reformer.

Professor Wolff addressed the entire audience as he was interviewed by the children. He was a positive role model to all those gathered and ensured that our proposed pilot programme presented older members as people who have made, and continue to make, positive contributions to society. His talk and the children's dance and song ensured that everyone was engaged and able to enjoy a social time together. The children later invited Professor Wolff and some MHA Northwood Live at Home Scheme members to a school assembly.

The AGM and launch were most certainly educational experiences, as children learned about officer and budget reports as well as the election of committee members (all kept brief). Interactive contributions from the children and Professor Wolff's talk added energy and enthusiasm to proceedings.

How did the pilot work?

So where did we start on the interventions? We began by listening to our Live at Home members and in so doing realized that smart phones and iPads were being bought for them, yet often they did not know how to use them.

It was clear that one area of educational progress which has widened the gap between young and old has been technology. Children can be observed swiping books, expecting pages to change before they are two years of age, as they are so used to electronic digital devices. Some parents and grandparents are learning Information Technology (IT) from young people they have contact with. Some children find it hard to imagine a world when there was no mobile phone and you had to queue at a red phone box in the street and insert coins to speak to a friend or family member. For this reason, we began our project by offering an informal social learning session with iPads.

A group of six to eight Year 5 children came and sat in pairs alongside an older person and began to show them how the iPad was switched on and various things it could do. Through conversation they ascertained what was of interest to the older person and then spent time showing them how to use the iPad. They were observed looking at maps, taking photos, sending emails, showing how to order products and using FaceTime. This resulted in some members being able to FaceTime relatives on the other side of the world, seeing real-time images of children and grandchildren, ordering goods online when they felt unwell or unable to go out for any reason, and reading books where they can increase the font size as eyesight diminishes.

We listened to what children said to members and what members said to children, and aimed to create a safe place for this mutual learning and social experience. We asked members and children for their ideas about multi-generational activities and used their comments to inform forward planning. In these pilot sessions we documented the types of questions older members asked, talked about what words mean to different generations and observed levels of social interaction and engagement. We also noted unintended learning outcomes and took opportunities to add quality to the children's learning and encourage reflection, questioning and empathy.

On the following page there are some reflections from the children when asked about co-designing or co-working with older people:

■ I have learned that older people are not as boring as you think but very interesting, smart and really funny, not to mention really kind.

We can learn how to behave, knitting and learn about places, and they can learn about technology, dance, music and trends.

Younger people can learn about mistakes the elderly made so we can avoid those in life ahead.

I have learned that teaching the elderly is beneficial and that they know a lot and can share a lot of knowledge.

We can learn things from wisdom and experience.

Participant members were very impressed with the children's ease of navigating iPads and smart phones and could see their skills and comfort levels were very high – the children had grown up in an era surrounded by technology. As Prensky (2001) explains, young people are 'native speakers of the digital language of computers, video games and social media', whereas those less familiar with technology are 'digital immigrants'. Our programme aimed to reduce this gap in understanding, and 39 older people benefited from this aspect of our pilot intervention. Steps taken in planning this project incorporated:

- purchasing iPads
- negotiating times with school and members
- agreeing which children to involve
- parental consent forms
- ensuring staff responsible had first-aid and safeguarding training
- including the offer to the MHA Northwood Live at Home programme
- recruiting volunteers who could sustain sessions during school holidays
- securing a suitable venue and resources
- pre- and post-evaluation
- monitoring (register, observation sessions)
- social informal learning session activities
- organizing refreshments
- funding the work.

Funding and resourcing

This work has been supported by the Heathrow Community Fund, Yeading Junior School, the MHA, the London Borough of Hillingdon and other funding sources reported in the 2015, 2016 and 2017 MHA Northwood Live at Home Scheme's Annual Reports. All funding received supports the charity's core programme, of which this multi-generational offer is one part. Our aim is to make this approach sustainable by working with more local schools and businesses to secure ongoing funding, to work with volunteers of all ages, and to reach more older people experiencing loneliness and/or social isolation. We note that, besides funding, logistics can be challenging – that is, ensuring that enough members are supported to come to each session (e.g. with transport), whilst respecting their right to choose.

Ongoing evaluation

Gathering evidence on the effects of social investment is often complex and substantially qualitative and anecdotal. *A Guide to Social Return on Investment* (Nicholls *et al.* 2012) provides a blank impact map and guide through scoping, stakeholders, mapping outcomes, identifying inputs and evidencing outcomes. Our ability to develop and deploy measures to evaluate this aspect of our work has been limited by available staff time and the need to sustain the wider social programme for our older members. Nonetheless, we take every opportunity to capture feedback from children and older people, given these constraints, and categorize recorded evidence by distinguishing between *activities, outputs, outcomes* and *impact*. The remainder of this chapter reports findings using this framework.

Activities

Tools used to measure activities were attendance sheets and activity evaluation sheets for levels of participation. The number of older people wanting to learn how to use the iPad over the three-year period was 39, supported by nine adult volunteers. Six primary school children attended each week during term time. Even though learning IT skills was life-changing for some members, it was also clear that others wanted to come to meet the children and IT was of secondary importance. Attendance levels dropped once members acquired skills and gained sufficient confidence to operate their own iPad or phone. Others found operating the technology too complex.

However, this IT-focused pilot developed into a more general free-choice session, with a range of activities available. Therefore, the children, young and older people were encouraged to use the iPads and time together to plan, co-design and engage in activities where the outcome was that of mutual benefit and learning. Ideas generated were then used to inform the multi-generational offer on the MHA Northwood Live at Home Scheme quarterly programme. These ideas included shared trips to the seaside, theatres, museums and informal social times as children came to perform, play games or stay and chat over weekly lunches. Children and members still meet weekly during term time and the range of activities and number of people and schools now involved has grown substantially.

As part of monitoring, we record the gender, nationality and languages used of all participants, and our aim is to develop mutually rewarding opportunities which focus on positive outcomes for all. This data is documented and reviewed to inform the extent to which we are bringing attitudinal change, increasing social contact between cultures and generations, and overcoming practical barriers to multi-generational engagement.

Outputs

To measure outputs and assess what happened as a result of our sessions, we conducted focused discussions with members and children over time and listened to what participants said. After interventions, the adults – usually a member of the school staff and the member of staff team from the charity present – discuss levels of interaction between young and old.

There have been occasions when children focused more on the activity they had elected to do, such as when they were making cards to send to Bulgaria with gifts that had been collected by their classmates and our scheme members. On another occasion, two boys were more interested in the game they were playing than in talking to or including older people. Gentle reminders to engage with older people were occasionally made but rarely required. Staff observed the developing relationships and affection children and members began to express to each other, which were often very obvious as they entered the room and as they departed.

After a series of interventions, we ask such evaluative questions as:

- What have you learnt about?
- What you have learnt/enjoyed most?
- How did you find the contact with the young/old person?

- What type of things did you do/research together?
- Is there anything you would change?
- Was there anything you found difficult?

These questions are used with some participants from each of the groups who have been engaged, both children and members. Below are some of the responses gathered.

In an initial discussion with a Year 5 boy, when asked why he had volunteered, he answered:

When you teach someone something it puts a smile on someone's face. I am good at using an iPad, so putting two and two together, I volunteered.

When asked what he hoped to learn through these sessions, he replied:

I hope to learn stuff from their generation, and I can teach them about mine.

When asked what he thought they might need to learn, he said:

How to FaceTime their families, online shopping, how to use settings. Some might like to play games.

A Year 5 girl added:

How to use YouTube, how to use the camera, how to use Google maps.

When asked if meeting our members had changed their views in any way, a Year 5 boy responded:

Yes, I think that the older people deserve the same stuff we have, for example, laptops and computers.

When asked what they had learned today, one 9-year-old girl said:

Old people are cool and fun... I used to think older people weren't really into these things but it turns out they are.

Another Year 5 girl said:

▨ The older people had style.

Over the series of sessions, children became increasingly comfortable talking and listening to the adults, and personal relationships were developing. This was evidenced by the fact that if someone was unable to come due to illness or a clash in commitments, children were enquiring about them by name.

Adult volunteers present at some multi-generational sessions captured incidents that demonstrate impact at an individual/group level. Some observations made at iPad sessions include:

- a member planning their route on public transport to a hospital appointment
- a mother looking up the house her son was planning to buy in another part of the country
- trying to source a winter coat 'but they are all too short and have padded shoulders'
- someone ordering a toy for a friend's cat
- enlarging a map of France for a member and talking about places they had both travelled to
- looking up types of birds and wild flowers.

One male member came with his sporting medals and shared programmes he had collected in his younger days (e.g. one from the FIM Speedway Championship in 1960 and another from ice hockey at Wembley in 1961). He stated, 'I don't want to learn the iPad, I just came to show them my sporting stuff' and proceeded to sit and talk to the children about ice hockey and motorbike racing. On one evaluation, a Year 5 boy wrote:

▨ Sometimes the elderly talk about when they were young, and it catches my attention because I love sports.

One member reported she had learned how to use FaceTime, the Apps store, how to connect to Wi-Fi, YouTube and BBC iPlayer, as well as how to delete, and commented that it was 'an excellent experience – I hope I can remember everything'. Another member said it was a 'perfect afternoon' in which she had enjoyed the girls' company. One girl she had worked with wrote:

> I enjoyed seeing my lady and taking pictures with her. I enjoyed it and thought she and all the other ladies were very nice and it was extremely fun.

All evaluation comments, ideas and views were analyzed and assessed by staff in the school and by a charity staff member to consider which activities offered the greatest opportunities for learning and were deemed relatively safe and affordable for all concerned. Feedback was actively encouraged. This was frequently verbal as the members and children often preferred to talk rather than write. On occasion we would ask children to interview each other for feedback in pairs, which develops their relationship and communication skills as well as providing insight into what they were learning and enjoying.

Multi-generational communication

Effective communication can be challenging, as children do not necessarily understand some expressions or life experiences older people refer to, and vice versa. Some illustrations of unfamiliar language and expressions we captured are as follows:

Year 5 boy

> What did she mean when she called me a smart chappie?

Female member

> The only App I know is a letter of application and as for a menu I thought you only got them when you went out for a meal somewhere.

Female member

> The only telephone I knew when I was growing up was in a red telephone box at the end of the village and you had to feed it with money. Now all young people seem to have their own mobile phones and they don't know how different it was when we were growing up.

Male member

■ What do you mean when you say scroll down, and what exactly is a website? Makes me think of spiders.

One member talked about how, when she was a headteacher, PE lessons took about half a day. A boy's response was 'That sounds great but why did they take so long?' She went on to explain how children stripped down to their pants and vest and they needed to ensure that everyone managed to put the right clothes back on. The child exclaimed, 'I think that is highly inappropriate!' Another member interjected and explained how she used to sew on embroidered badges to make sure her children came home with the right clothes, which led to the question 'What does "embroidered" mean?'

Children learned about how life was in the past, but certain expressions needed clarification (e.g. 'What do you mean by a "ration book"?' 'What exactly do you mean by an "Anderson shelter"?').

When discussing games with an older male member, one Year 5 boy assumed he was talking about video and IT games, not cricket and rugby. The member thought this boy was describing gaming, as in gambling. It took more time and questioning to clarify what meaning they were both trying to convey.

Children would sometimes be misunderstood by members who struggled to hear, especially if the children were quietly spoken. This was something we talked to the children about. We encouraged them to project their voices or to move and sit away from others, so there was less background noise. Children were, however, never out of sight from the adults responsible.

Outcomes

Outcomes are changes or consequences of involvement for stakeholders, which can be observed about three months after activities have occurred. This could be attitudinal change or a measured change in behaviour (e.g. increased access to social groups). Besides the joy or pleasure experienced from encounters at the time, it is important we note and consider collateral benefit; that is, the positive ripple or knock-on effect of these experiences.

When people shift their understanding and perception, it can have a wider effect on their families and communities, as one Year 5 boy commented:

> Now when I see an older person in the street, I know they are real people, people with interests and their own story to tell. Before they were just old people.

Reflections from older people expressed similar shifts in attitudes, as one reported:

> The young people were so polite and respectful; I didn't quite expect that, they were delightful.

The Live at Home programme offer for older members has been significantly enhanced by the ideas generated and we are providing more opportunities for continuing safe social contact across the generations. Children, young and older people were all invited to discuss potential ideas for trips and activities, and the outcome from this helps shape our programme.

One lady attended several iPad sessions and then had a gap and went off on holiday. She joined us several weeks later when we presented certificates to children who had helped. She was remembered by a young girl, who called her by name and asked how her holiday had been. Given the time lapse involved, this demonstrates good active listening, recall and interest on the part of the child, which certainly delighted our member. This child was recognized in school in front of peers for her attention to detail and good people skills. Such positive affirmation of individuals is having an impact on the school ethos, and this role modelling has encouraged others to want to volunteer to come and meet older people in this way.

Impact

Impact captures the bigger picture of changes such as decrease in number of people feeling lonely or socially isolated after an intervention. The National Foundation for Educational Research (NFER) published a report entitled *Intergenerational Practice: Outcomes and Effectiveness* and concluded that this is complex and not easy to get right or to demonstrate conclusively. Key considerations noted were: the preparation time, the potential to reinforce negative stereotypes if things go wrong, and the need to have skilled staff who can deal with the unexpected (Martin, Springate and Atkinson 2010).

In this pilot, multi-generational programme, the learning has been mutually beneficial to both young and older people. There have been issues about transport and low numbers of older people on occasion, or times when it has proved difficult for the school to release children. However, the positive benefits to all concerned made it a valuable journey with no evidence of negative outcomes in terms of attitudes to young or older people.

The NFER (Springate, Atkinson and Martin 2010) also reviewed literature around intergenerational practice and identified the following six key factors for success: Sustainability, Staffing, Participants, Activities, Organization and Partnerships. It is our intention to continue the learning journey into the future and continue to *plan, execute, review* and *reflect* together on the extent to which interventions add benefit for all involved.

As a result of our pilot work, we have seen significant engagement with other local schools. The Local Support Committee are very positive about this development and the way it offers a means of building capacity for promoting social contact and improving mental health outcomes for children, young and older people. As a result of telling other schools about our pilot of multi-generational experiences, the work has been scaled up to include more schools. Secondary school students from Northwood College have interviewed our members to canvass their ideas and preferences. Several other local schools have engaged in our multi-generational work by collecting gifts for harvest festivals and Christmas and inviting members into their school settings. Two local primary schools and a further secondary school have invited our members into school and entertained them, provided refreshments and expressed interest in this being an ongoing partnership.

Some examples of how the programme was further developed are:

- Yeading Junior School children joined some members on their annual scheme holiday, where together we visited Eastbourne Pier.
- Children and Northwood Live at Home members enjoyed refreshments at the Victorian tea shop.
- Two children were looking forward to meeting a particular lady they had met through the iPad training. Regrettably, due to ill-health this person was unable to go, so these two 10-year-olds bought a bracelet gift for her, which is an indicator of kindness and compassion: a school virtue in action. This act of kindness made a significant impression on the shopkeeper, who gave the girls a free gift, which illuminates the ripple effect or collateral benefit.

When asked to pick a word to describe the trip to Eastbourne, one child said 'breath-taking' and another 'magnificent'. When asked 'What would you change about the day?', responses were 'Make it longer or even a residential so we could have two days there' and 'Nothing, it was perfect.'

Whilst reflecting on the Eastbourne trip with six children, there was a moment of realization from one boy that they had influenced the decision to go. The delight in recognizing they had affected the programme was obvious. This is an illustration of a child waking up to the fact that he can influence what happens and, by working as a team, the group could shape events, developing some understanding of democratic influence.

Oh, yes...so it was because of us that our whole class got to go to the seaside, and we said museum too and we said about eating together and going to the theatre. You asked for our ideas and that's why we went.

Based upon research that participating in cultural events enhances wellbeing, the Northwood Live at Home members enjoyed a performance of songs from the *Lion King* by Year 4 children. This was inspirational, energetic and colourful and the clapping indicated that it was much appreciated by over 30 people. At another lunch, children provided entertainment with dances and then explained to our members what being an 'Agent of Social Change' was. They shared many of the social action campaigns they had been working on, such as 'Walk for Water' and 'Homelessness', and included the Christmas social action our members had also participated in. This was the collection of items for Christmas boxes distributed by Trussell Trust UK and the Foundation of Social Change and Inclusion (FSCI), which works with vulnerable young people in Bulgaria and other Balkan countries. Yeading Junior School collected items to fill 144 Christmas boxes, and the Northwood Live at Home members worked with other local faith groups, adding another 30, which contributed toward the 11,000 that were transported. Children and older members were thinking globally and acting locally on social justice issues, which is a Public Health England approach also adopted by the WE movement.

Singing, theatre, physical activity and eating are regular offerings to our members, and we are now working to include opportunities for these to be multi-generational. Therefore, the Northwood Live at Home Scheme included 15 children on a trip to the Royal Albert Hall to hear Symphonic Rock. Children who had some interest or talent were offered this opportunity in the hope that it would be inspirational and motivating for them. This proved to be an experience they thoroughly enjoyed and enthused about to our members as they chatted to them on the return journey. Interestingly, when we entered the building, our group was split up and channelled to different doors by a member of staff there, possibly an indication that in the UK we increasingly want to keep generations apart rather than encourage interaction and integration. As we had purchased group tickets for this multi-generational group, we did all manage to sit together and the incident did not prevent us from sharing a wonderful time.

Parents have been very supportive of what we are seeking to accomplish and none of them have objected to children being out of school, as exemplified by the comment, 'I hope that my daughter can continue to come to the Mix and Mingle sessions with Northwood Live at Home – she has grown in confidence hugely as a result of doing this.' Evaluations from members and children have also been overwhelmingly positive, and whilst it is hard to know how to measure smiles on faces or quantify growth in character virtues, there are indicators and evidence that wellbeing for all generations is being enhanced. There has been a cultural shift toward this multi-generational approach within our partnership that we hope to build upon further as we continue our learning journey.

Next steps

At a time when loneliness is increasingly recognized as having an impact on the mental health of young and older people, and developing character is important in preparing children for adult life, there is a place for schools to work with local communities to explore partnerships for mutual benefit. We face the prospect of many people living longer with less social support from immediate families, so finding innovative ways to increase safe and sustainable social contact between generations will be important if we are to make best use of our local resources.

Our aim is to develop partnerships with local schools who want to engage with older local people to strengthen multi-generational friendships and utilize our resources, people and places to best effect. A sense of place and belonging are key to young people's mental health (Kane and Bibby 2018), and building bridges between generations will enhance perceptions of safety and purpose in any given community. Our older residents are a resource in terms of experience and can sometimes be those with more time to listen and engage with younger people; also, children have brought great moments of joy to many of our members. We plan to create more opportunities for this to keep happening and continue to learn by doing. Multi-generational contact zones in local libraries, youth centres and schools with effective safeguarding processes in place could provide a way forward, but it will require attitudinal change in how we train staff, use buildings and engage with local communities.

At WE Day 2019, 12,000 young people were celebrating volunteering efforts and five of our volunteers were on the stage representing Yeading Junior School, four of whom had been volunteers with the MHA Northwood Live at Home Scheme, so we know they earned the right to be there. Our hope is that the MHA and schools can work collaboratively in local areas across the nation to create opportunities for safe multi-generational contact. We are training the next generation of educators, carers and parents, so it is worth investment if we are seeking to improve community relations and understanding.

The health of young people is one of the biggest assets any country can have; it constitutes the future. Young people need to grow in the knowledge they are valued by the older generation, just as older people need to be engaged in shaping their communities and respected for the insight and experience their lives have given them. Our multi-generational pilot programme was opportunistic and very local; what is required now is for a more systemic approach that releases the positive potential of people and place to cross the generational and cultural divide we have currently created.

References

Arthur, J., Kristjansson, K., Walker, D., Sanderse, W. and Jones, C. (2015) *Character Education in UK Schools*. Birmingham: The Jubilee Centre for Character and Virtues (University of Birmingham). Accessed 27/01/19 at www.jubileecentre.ac.uk

Beth Johnson Foundation (2011) *A Guide to Intergenerational Practice*. Stoke-on-Trent: Beth Johnson Foundation. Accessed 28/02/19 at www.ageingwellinwales.com/Libraries/Documents/Guide-to-Intergenerational-Practice.pdf

Green, M., Iparraguirre, J., Davidson, S., Rossall, P. and Zaidi, A. (2017) *A Summary of Age UK's Index of Wellbeing in Later Life*. London: Age UK. Accessed 28/01/19 at www.ageuk.org.uk/documents/EN-GB/For-professionals/Research/AgeUK-Wellbeing-Index-Summary-web.pdf?dtrk=true

Holmes, P. and Thompson, L. (2018) *Tackling Loneliness and Social Isolation: The Role of Commissioners*. Social Care Institute for Excellence (SCIE) Highlights No 3. Accessed 28/02/19 at www.scie.org.uk/files/prevention/connecting/loneliness-social-isolation/tackling-loneliness-and-social-isolation.pdf

Holt-Lunstad, J., Smith, T., Baker, M., Harris, T. and Stephenson, D. (2015) 'Loneliness and social isolation as risk factors for mortality.' *Perspectives on Psychological Science 10*(2), 227–237.

Intergenerational Foundation (2016) *Generations Apart: The Growth of Age Segregation in England and Wales*. London: Intergenerational Foundation. Accessed 05/05/19 at www.if.org.uk/wp-content/uploads/2016/09/Generations-Apart-Brochure.pdf

Kane, M. and Bibby, J. (2018) *A Place to Grow: Exploring the Future Health of Young People in Five Sites across the UK*. The Health Foundation. Accessed 12/03/19 at www.health.org.uk/publications/a-place-to-grow

Kingman, D. (2016) *Generations Apart? The Growth of Age Segregation in England and Wales*. London: Intergenerational Foundation. Accessed 08/10/19 at www.if.org.uk/wp-content/uploads/2016/09/Generations-Apart_Report_Final_Web-Version-1.pdf

Leventhal, T. and Brooks-Gunn, J. (2000) 'The neighborhoods they live in: The effects of neighborhood residence on child and adolescent outcomes'. *Psychological Bulletin 126*(2), pp. 309–337. Accessed 21/12/18 at https://pdfs.semanticscholar.org/4eda/5c77f111bde4d82017af464c0278c7ed4c59.pdf

Marsh, S. (2018) 'Combat loneliness with "social prescribing", says Theresa May'. *The Guardian*, 14 October. Accessed 26/01/19 at www.theguardian.com/society/2018/oct/14/loneliness-social-prescribing-theresa-may

Martin, K., Springate, I. and Atkinson, M. (2010) *Intergenerational Practice: Outcomes and Effectiveness* (LGA Research Report). Slough: NFER. Accessed 28/02/19 at https://files.eric.ed.gov/fulltext/ED511391.pdf

National Audit Office (2006) *Delivering Efficiently: Strengthening the Links in Public Service Delivery Chains*. London: National Audit Office and Audit Commission.

Nicholls, J., Lawlor, E., Neitzert, E. and Goodspeed, T. (2012) *A Guide to Social Return on Investment*. London: Office of the Third Sector, Cabinet Office.

Office for National Statistics (ONS) (2018a) *Measuring National Well-being: Quality of Life in the UK*. Accessed 25/05/19 at www.ons.gov.uk/peoplepopulationandcommunity/wellbeing/articles/measuringnationalwellbeing/qualityoflifeintheUK2018

Office for National Statistics (ONS) (2018b) *National Measurement of Loneliness*. Accessed 25/05/19 at www.ons.gov.uk/peoplepopulationandcommunity/wellbeing/compendium/nationalmeasurementofloneliness/2018

Prensky, M. (2001) 'Digital natives, digital immigrants'. *On the Horizon 9*(5), 1–6. Accessed 17/01/19 at www.marcprensky.com/writing/Prensky%20-%20Digital%20Natives,%20Digital%20Immigrants%20-%20Part1.pdf

Springate, I., Atkinson, M. and Martin, K. (2008) *Intergenerational Practice: A Review of the Literature* (LGA Research Report F/SR262). Slough: NFER. Accessed 28/02/19 at www.nfer.ac.uk/publications/LIG01/LIG01.pdf

Van Willigen, M. (2000) 'Differential benefits of volunteering across the life course'. *The Journals of Gerontology. Series B: Psychological Sciences and Social Sciences 55*(5), 308–318.

Voce, A. (2008) 'Risky play prepares kids for life'. *The Guardian*, 6 August. Accessed 28/02/19 at www.theguardian.com/society/2008/aug/06/children.play

Chapter 6

Character Education within the 'Me Zone'

JEAN-MICHEL BALLAY IN CONSULTATION WITH THE CHILDREN AND FAMILIES TEAM

This chapter will discuss some of the work that we carry out in the 'Me Zone', an area in school which is a nurturing environment for the children, and which is facilitated by our Children and Families team. The idea of the name Me Zone followed the statement 'looking after the whole of me', indicating that this area in school is not only supporting the children's academic needs but also their social and emotional needs, with the aim of enhancing positive mental health for all.

Within our team we have a school social worker, two learning mentors, and a home–school worker. The idea of having an internal support team originated when the local authority provided an opportunity for Yeading Junior School to have a social work student unit onsite. This means that throughout each academic year the school has a number of students on placement, from shadowing opportunities to 100-day placements whereby they can work with key children in groups and on a one-to-one basis, offering support to children and their families. From this, the internal Children and Families team, who work with the social and emotional needs of children, has continued to develop, alongside the high-priority agenda for children's mental health.

The character virtues we will be addressing within our chapter are compassion, reflection and resilience, and we explore how these are used daily within our work through group and one-to-one interventions with children. We will discuss the key interventions that we facilitate, including: the Marlborough Project; Yoga; Seasons for Growth; Calming Group; and one-to-one direct work which incorporates both drop-in sessions and the

Self-Esteem Group. These programmes are based on early intervention and are there to support the children with developing the necessary skills to aid them in accessing the curriculum more effectively. The programmes are also aimed at making a positive impact in terms of the children's social and emotional needs, ensuring that they are happy in and outside of school and therefore emotionally ready to learn.

Within each section we will discuss how we support the children to be equipped with the skills to continue to develop through the different stages of their lives. As all children are different, some children may be able to vocalize their feelings and emotions, whereas others may find this more difficult and could present as quite closed when it comes to accessing interventions. It is important not to push the child into accessing support if they are not ready; however, we would always encourage the child to recognize that the space is there for them and they can choose to leave whenever they wish. This usually supports the child to feel safe, knowing they have an exit strategy if any feelings become overwhelming. As facilitators, it is very important to be in tune with your listening and observational skills during all sessions. Although some children may not present as very vocal, sometimes these children can tell you more about how they are feeling through their body language and use of play than others who may be verbal communicators (Dunhill, Elliot and Shaw 2009).

As these programmes are of a sensitive nature and the examples we have are real-life cases, we will only be sharing generic information here to ensure that identification cannot be linked to any specific child or family. We will address relevant theories that apply within our practice and will explain how we have embedded compassion, reflection and resilience throughout the identified programmes.

Emotional wellbeing interventions
The Marlborough Project

The Marlborough Project[1] is a reflective programme where we are looking at 'the whole of the child', including their family and home environment. As a school we understand the importance of engaging parents and

1   Adapted from the work advanced by Asen, E., Dawson, N. and McHugh, B. (2001) *Multiple Family Therapy: The London Marlborough Model and its Wider Applications.* London: H. Karnac (Books) Ltd.

children together in order to achieve positive outcomes for the child both at home and at school. During previous programmes, when we worked with the children only, we found that some of the children were making certain disclosures of events that took place at home and which may have contradicted the virtues we were promoting at school. Due to this, we realized the importance of bringing parents and children together because in order for children to achieve the best possible outcomes, we need to be working alongside their parents with the same goals and aspirations in mind.

Children and families that engage with this programme are identified through three separate processes. It may be that the child's behaviour is of concern in school and we have identified that they may find it hard to self-regulate and manage their emotions in a safe way. In a case such as this we would liaise with the parents about what we have observed and, in some cases, it may be that the parents have identified similar difficulties at home. Through discussions with parents, we would inform and encourage them to take part in the Marlborough Project so as to assist their child with learning coping strategies, and also for them to liaise with other parents whose children may also be going through similar changes whereby positive parenting strategies can be shared. Another way in which families are identified to take part in the programme could be that the family is already being supported through statutory intervention, such as children's social care or Special Educational Needs (SEN), and the programme would assist in supporting the family alongside the statutory plan in place. An example of this may be where the child's low self-esteem has been identified as an additional factor alongside the core concerns for the child; therefore, in the statutory plan, we would look for ways to improve this and may therefore suggest that the parent and child engage in the Marlborough Project as one intervention that could work towards achieving the desired outcome. In cases such as these we would be required to feed back to the relevant services on any progress the child has made as well as the engagement of parents throughout the programme.

The maximum capacity for the Marlborough Project is four families, and it runs for one session a week for eight weeks. The aim of the programme is to strengthen the relationship between parent and child and to create a safe environment for the child to talk about their feelings and for the parents to share their difficulties. At the beginning of each session we always start by giving each member of the group their own 'emotions fan' which lists nine separate feelings, including proud, worried, thoughtful, angry, surprised, upset, happy, disappointed and other feeling. Each member is required to pick their feeling of the day and to talk about why they have picked this emotion. In our experience, this is a great way to open the group session as it empowers each member to identify how they are feeling and also lets us, as facilitators, know if there are any members of the group who are having a particularly difficult day. If this is the case, we make a mental note to allow time to go back to them at the end of our discussion to ensure they have sufficient time to talk and reflect. At this time they will be encouraged to think about what is working well and identify any possible solutions for moving forwards. This is based on facilitators using solution-focused practice – trying to empower the parent to focus all discussions on the potential solutions to their problem rather than on the problem itself (Teater 2014). The parent can also receive advice from other parents who may have experienced something similar and also ourselves, as and when it is necessary. If a parent appears distressed in any way or has a more sensitive issue to discuss, we will ensure that they are seen alone at the end of the session.

Towards the end of each session we incorporate an interactive play session between parent and child. This could include drawing, reading, games, and arts and crafts activities. In our experience it is important not to presume that all parents have learnt the skills of how to interact with their children through play. This programme creates an opportunity for parents to develop such skills within a non-threatening environment. For example, if any parent finds this activity particularly difficult, we are always on hand to encourage and, if necessary, to model and mirror positive play interaction to support the parent in feeling comfortable. To finish the session we set weekly targets for home and school, and work together to support the child in understanding their thoughts, feelings and actions, allowing them a platform to reflect and continue to build resilience. The home target is selected by the child and parent and is monitored by the parent. The parent is encouraged to be clear and descriptive about their expectations and to help the child understand what the consequence will be if they do not meet their target. The school target is set by the child, learning mentors and the class teacher. This is monitored weekly and any concerns can be identified through the target mark achieved, which is then fed back to parents during the weekly meeting. Some examples of home and school targets are shown in Table 6.1.

Table 6.1 Weekly target sheets for school and home

IN SCHOOL TARGETS	MON am	MON pm	TUE am	TUE pm	WED am	WED pm	THUR am	THUR pm	FRI am	FRI pm
Stay within class during learning time	2	3	3	3	4	3	4	4	3	2
Complete homework	1	1	3	3	3	3	3	3	4	4

AT HOME TARGETS	MON am	MON pm	TUE am	TUE pm	WED am	WED pm	THUR am	THUR pm	FRI am	FRI pm
Keep your room tidy	3	3	4	4	4	3	4	4	3	2
Listen to mum first time without her having to ask you again	4	2	3	4	4	3	3	2	3	2

Key: 4 – achieved all the time; 3 –achieved most of the time; 2 – achieved some of the time; 1 – not achieved.

Due to the sensitive nature of this programme we sometimes need to liaise with external agencies in order to support the family more effectively. For example, we have made referrals to the Educational Psychology service, school nurse team, parenting classes, and, Speech and Language service. These provisions are discussed with parents, since we work on a 'whole family approach' ensuring that parents have given consent and are involved in the entire process. We also liaise with children's social care, when necessary, regarding the progress of families, including the holistic view of the relationship between parent and child.

One challenge we have experienced when working in this way is that the parent may become over-reliant on the sessions or present their own needs over those of their child. In such instances, we would refer or signpost to other agencies specifically to target the parents' needs (e.g. Talking Therapies, Mind, Key Working Service). We have found it is paramount to be clear on the boundaries and expectations at the beginning of the eight weeks and to remind parents where necessary to ensure that the focus is on improving the outcomes for the child's overall wellbeing.

Yoga

At Yeading Junior School, we have a Community House, where parents can undertake courses such as English and Maths and Parenting, or study for National Vocational Qualifications (NVQs). The house is also used for daily coffee mornings in order to encourage community cohesion whereby parents meet and talk with other parents. One of the activities provided for parents is weekly yoga sessions. The parents enjoy this tremendously and feel it is very beneficial for stress relief. During parental feedback, parents said they felt yoga was something that would benefit their children, too, and this was therefore facilitated. The yoga programme has assisted children in developing calming techniques and coping strategies to manage anxiety, stress and overall mental health and wellbeing. They are selected to take part in this programme in liaison with the class teacher, parents and support staff. The criteria we use for participation involve identifying those children who may present as anxious or who worry about things which are out of their control.

The yoga programme lasts for ten weeks and is facilitated by an external agency. The aim of the yoga sessions is to support the children to develop better concentration, attention and focus, and to improve self-control and confidence. Although many of the benefits are internal, yoga can also assist with improving flexibility and posture. Most of the sessions are geared towards finding inner peace. The facilitator creates make-believe journeys which include obstacles for the children to overcome. Many of the children have reported noticing benefits when they become angry and are able to use the breathing techniques and strategies they have learnt to self-regulate and problem-solve. One of the things that needs to be considered when setting up this programme is the amount of space required to accommodate all of the yoga mats and resources.

Seasons for Growth

Seasons for Growth is a widely used programme which originated in Australia and has been cascaded all over the world (Graham 2008). Two members of staff were trained to facilitate Seasons for Growth within Yeading Junior School and it has been ongoing there ever since. The programme is used to address any changes that a child may have gone through that could create anxiety for them (e.g. bereavement, new sibling, change of school, moving home, etc.). The children are individually selected to take part and sometimes may be referred by parents. The programme runs once a week, for ten weeks, and is framed around the process of acceptance whereby the children are able to link their thoughts and feelings to the changes within their own bodies and to recognize how these are displayed through behaviour. The maximum number of children selected to participate is eight, due to the sensitivity of the programme. Sometimes the resources that are provided need to be tailored to the individual group to ensure that they gain the most from each session. Prior to starting the session, we will always discuss confidentiality within the group to ensure that there is a safe environment for the children to discuss their feelings. We also inform the children that whenever they feel the need to talk outside of the group, they can do this by coming to talk with one of the facilitators in private.

The focus in all sessions is around changes the children go through in their lives, from birth to the present, and the feelings that come with this. This is demonstrated through looking at the four yearly weather seasons: Winter, Spring, Summer and Autumn. Unlike the other programmes we facilitate, this particular programme focuses on the use of visuals and physical resources to bring it alive and for the children to be actively engaged with the activity, as they are able to relate the changes discussed with their everyday lives. An example of this might be one session where we use leaves to represent the effects of the changing seasons: from the leaves growing in the Spring to them falling off the trees in Autumn and then re-growing again. This helps the children to understand the cycle of change and the acceptance that comes with this.

Because of the sensitive nature of the programme, the Seasons for Growth sessions are always run by two members of staff. This ensures that if a child becomes distressed or emotional, one member of staff can stay with the group while the other can support the young person who is upset until they are ready to return to the group.

Each week the children complete their own Seasons for Growth booklet, which captures their feelings towards the change they have experienced and the emotions that come with it. The booklet is shared with parents at the end of the ten weeks to encourage the parents to continue the discussions with their children and to assist them in working through the change they have experienced. Sometimes the parents may be unaware, or not realize the significance, of the impact the change is having on their child. On sharing the booklets, we usually encourage parents to come back and see us if they have any questions or queries regarding the work undertaken. On some occasions the child may decide they do not wish to take their book home, and in such instances we would always respect the child's wishes; however, the reason for this would be explored. In a situation like this we would agree with the child a safe place to keep their booklet in school so that if they wish to revisit their work, they have the opportunity to do so.

Calming Group

The Calming Group is based upon age-appropriate anger management skills. We complete an assessment (in school within the Me Zone) of the child's needs, interviewing both the child and all staff members who work with them. Based on the outcome, we will then decide whether the child would benefit more from one-to-one or group sessions.

The Calming Group has a clear direction, with a beginning, a middle and an end, and progress is monitored throughout. We monitor the child's progress by asking them to complete a pre-course assessment, to enable us to understand their level of need; the assessment is then repeated on completion of the Calming Group intervention. Sessions can be adapted to suit the needs of the group and we ensure that we incorporate a session of reflection, whereby the children take part in problem-solving activities and role play to experience how people may feel when they are around someone who is displaying behaviour that challenges. This supports the children in developing compassion and empathy for others, which we would like to believe helps to equip them with the skills and value-set necessary for a successful and happy future.

We also try to ensure that the children learn the difference between emotion and behaviour, and how it is perfectly normal to experience anger as long as we express it in a safe and healthy way. We would then take time to discuss proactive strategies and reactive strategies, such as the use of breathing techniques, building a feelings vocabulary and taking time out, so that the child is equipped with their own toolbag of coping mechanisms for instances when the anger emotion may arise. What may work for one child does not necessarily work for another and so it is very important that we track and measure the impact on the children individually. We do this through discussions with parents and teachers, and the use of 'before and after' intervention questionnaires, tracking whether there has been a reduction in the number of incident slips; we also speak to the child directly. It is worth mentioning here that in the case of the children we support on a one-to-one basis due to their level of anger, we continually evaluate their progress to identify when is the right time to reintegrate them back into the group. There may be different timescales for each child; however, we will always ensure that we do this to encourage collaborative learning and for the individual development of their peer-to-peer social skills.

The Self-Esteem Group

The Self-Esteem programme has a very sensitive selection process whereby we identify children who may be vulnerable and overlooked as they manage to mask their emotions and difficulties. Sometimes children are also identified to take part through the transition process into Yeading Junior School (we are notified that the child would benefit from this support or that they have already been receiving it in their previous school, but it did not come to a closure).

The Self-Esteem programme is based on supporting the children to build resilience and confidence within themselves, and their emotional wellbeing is closely monitored. We encourage children to build on their social skills and to go out of their comfort zone in activities such as role play, debating, drama, dance and problem-solving. This is to promote their growth and resilience in being able to handle life challenges and conflict.

This programme is child-focused and sometimes it can be led by the children, which also empowers them to self-solve and develop their leadership skills.

We measure the impact of this programme through monitoring pupil behaviour, their future expectations, pupil attendance that was of a previous concern, and the increase of children's confidence and perception of self. At the beginning of the first session we ask each child to complete a self-evaluation form. This looks at the child's strengths and difficulties and is completed again at the end of the eight weeks, so that we can measure and monitor progress effectively. We also liaise with parents and class teachers to gain feedback regarding any changes that have been observed by them; this is in addition to the observations of Me Zone staff not only when working within groups, but also their observations of these same children during break and at other times during the school day.

Some children find it difficult to work within a group and therefore we offer some one-to-one sessions for these identified children. The referrals for children to participate in one-to-one support could come from parents, teachers or external agencies such as children's social care; however, parents would always be notified and their agreement sought. This would usually be when there is a sensitive issue the child or family is working through, and because of confidentiality it would not be appropriate to discuss these feelings within a group environment. Within the one-to-one sessions, we support children to work through many changes or difficulties they are experiencing in their lives (e.g. bereavement, family separation, family crisis, anxiety, anger management, living with parental substance misuse, living with parental mental health difficulties, etc.). Due to their sensitive nature we always hold our one-to-one sessions in a separate confidential space away from the groups and drop-in sessions. This is to avoid any interruptions which could disrupt the flow and to ensure that the child feels safe to discuss any potentially difficult topics.

Another reason a child may be considered for one-to-one support is if they have accessed a group and it has become apparent that they may negatively influence or change the dynamics of that group and thus would benefit more from a one-to-one intervention. An example of this was a child who would manipulate situations and other children to do things for her. This would usually be displayed through escalation of voice and commandments to other children who might appear vulnerable. It was evident that this was a skill the child had learnt and developed to get their needs met, regardless of the impact this might have on others.

Therefore, it was decided that the child was not ready to access a group environment and one-to-one support was put in place to try to address this and provide the child with other strategies to get their needs met and to acknowledge the impact this behaviour was having on others around them.

One of the activities that was used in a session was the 'feelings onion' (Tait and Wosu 2013, p.95). The idea is to draw the onion, showing all of its layers and talking about feelings and/or behaviour. The idea is that the outside of the onion is how the world may see you; however when you look inside, you can see that the onion has many layers. The outside layers may be what friends at school see, and the inner layers may be only what your family see or what you know about yourself. The idea of this activity is to work through the multiple layers of the onion by talking about how the child feels around friends, at school, with family, at home, and when alone. As a feeling is identified, the facilitator discusses this feeling with the young person and expands upon why they feel that emotion and how this is portrayed through their behaviour. In our experience, this activity may take longer than one session since with each identified emotion, time needs to be taken to fully explore this, including the environment the child is in when the feeling arises, the impact on themselves when they feel this way, and also the impact on people around them. If it is found that the impact on others is negative, we spend some time exploring other ways to express their feelings, which helps them to maintain positive relationships they have built with others.

When working on a one-to-one basis with a child, the initial two or three sessions are focused on relationship-building to ensure that the child feels comfortable and gets to know the adult within a safe and professional environment. This allows sufficient time for the facilitator to find out the child's likes and dislikes, which will always be used to inform the choice of resources to be used in the sessions going forward. Although this is done to assist with planning the sessions, there is always an element of flexibility and, if the child wants to access other resources available to them, they are encouraged to do so.

As we like to place a focus on child-centred practice during our sessions (Foley and Leverett 2008), we do not always view ourselves as the lead and so try to ensure that we are doing more active listening than talking and that the communication is based on the child's terms and not just our own. We would always consider not just their interest but also the age of the child and their developmental ability. Some of the resources we use during sessions include arts and crafts, drawing, board games, storytelling with the use of puppets, feeling cards, etc. The one-to-one sessions are reviewed regularly and the number of sessions are flexible depending on the child's needs.

Parents are always informed and their consent is given prior to working with the child. Feedback on how the sessions are progressing will also be shared where appropriate with parents and external agencies. We always ensure that there is a clear beginning, a middle, and an end whereby the child has an appropriate closure and is able to own that by being part of the decision-making when they feel they no longer need the support. This empowers the child in moving forwards and developing the resilience needed for any future challenges. We inform the child that if they feel they need further support in the future, they can let us know, and we believe this allows the child to know they are being held in mind and therefore assists with a smooth closure.

Drop-in sessions

Although we have all of the set interventions above, we also allow time for what we call 'drop-in' sessions. This is where a child or adult may come unexpectedly with an issue or problem which needs resolving or to be worked through. Dependent upon the issues presented, we either deal with it immediately or allocate a time during the day to get back to them.

We have recognized that during playtime periods there is an increase in the number of drop-in cases and, on certain occasions, we have had to assess whether some of the concerns could be more appropriately managed by class teachers or lunchtime supervisors. This is to ensure that each child's concern is dealt with in a timely fashion each day and that no worries are taken home unresolved. This is the case normally when the concern is a playground dispute or a friendship issue.

Another type of drop-in we receive at lunchtime is from those children who dislike the outside lunchtime environment because of anxiety at being with unfamiliar children or in feeling overwhelmed by the large playground environment. These children are usually already accessing group work interventions for confidence and social skill development. In such circumstances, we usually set up free play in the Me Zone, where the child can access arts and crafts, Lego® or board games. We always encourage such children to bring a friend with them to the drop-in, so that we can informally observe their social skills and ongoing development, and ensure that they are interacting with peers of their own age and not just the adults present.

Occasionally, the other type of drop-in we receive is of a more serious nature, whereby there is a reported concern outside of school for a particular child. In instances such as these, we will always follow our safeguarding policy and procedures, including involving external agencies as and when necessary to ensure that the child's worry is dealt with appropriately and safely within an appropriate environment and timescale.

To conclude, we feel that incorporating the character virtues within our work has supported the whole school in working together in order to achieve positive social and emotional wellbeing for the 'whole of the child'. We feel that in order to embed the character virtues and solidify the importance of learning such skills, it is paramount for it to be a universal project and to be used throughout the school day, which is now a vision that has been achieved. Although this is now the case, the journey has not always been smooth sailing and it has taken hard work and commitment by all staff to embed the character virtues and to promote good moral character through all that we do. The interventions that we have discussed within this chapter have been adapted to suit our community and the needs of our families. Although the programmes and skills identified are transferrable to other school contexts, each school may feel the need to adapt the programmes we have presented so that they are more reflective of the particular needs of their own children, community and locality.

References

Dunhill, A., Elliott, B. and Shaw, A. (2009) *Effective Communication and Engagement with Children and Young People, Their Families and Carers*. Exeter: Learning Matters Ltd.

Foley, P. and Leverett, S. (2008) *Connecting with Children. Developing Working Relationships*. Bristol: The Policy Press.

Graham, A. (2008) *Seasons for Growth Companion Manual* (3rd edition). Sydney: The Mary Mackillop Foundation.

Tait, A. and Wosu, H. (2013) *Direct Work with Vulnerable Children: Playful Activities and Strategies for Communication*. London: Jessica Kingsley Publishers.

Teater, B. (2014) *An Introduction to Applying Social Work Theories and Methods* (2nd edition). Maidenhead: Open University Press.

Chapter 7

Financial Literacy and Character Education

DAVID MORAN AND CAROLE JONES

The teaching of Financial Education at Yeading Junior School is linked to the virtues that are embedded across the curriculum. The school is recognized as a Centre of Excellence by the charity Young Enterprise and Young Money (formerly known as the Personal Finance Education Group [pfeg]), having achieved this status in 2011 and 2014. Young Enterprise sets out to work directly with young people, their teachers and parents, businesses and influencers to build a successful and sustainable future for all young people and society at large. A Centre of Excellence for Financial Education is defined by Young Money in their booklet as follows:

> recognises and rewards schools who are committing to, developing and continuing excellence in financial education in their own school and beyond. The programme supports excellence in leadership and management of financial education. We will help you develop engaging and inspiring learning programmes, alongside comprehensive staff development and training. (Young Money 2018)

This chapter reflects on the journey of Financial Education within our school, the rationale for teaching this area, and the impact on the children, as well as how the school attained the status of Centre of Excellence.

Financial Education was introduced to the school at the time when the Extended School's initiative was being embedded and in conjunction with *Every Child Matters* (DfES, 2003) policy. The headteacher had been invited to a continuing (Continuing Professional Development [CPD]) presentation from a personal finance education consultancy and was impressed with the background of the pfeg organization alongside its programmes and therefore requested the consultant to deliver CPD to the whole staff team. A number of sessions were delivered, and the school established a very good, long-lasting relationship with the organization. The main focus of this training was to assist staff in understanding about children's view of money and their understanding of needs and wants. This dovetailed with the work that was already going on in Personal, Social, Health and Citizenship Education (PSHCE). A series of staff meeting sessions ensued with pfeg, and the school also actively engaged with the resources available in order to ensure continuity.

The staff and children became very innovative and embedded a new initiative across the school involving financial literacy. Children from Years 3 to 6 began to assist in the creation of a currency, led by a member of the teaching staff. This currency has continued to be in operation for more than ten years. Establishing this enterprise initiative was quite complex and involved considerable teamwork. A unit of currency had to be named and its value decided upon. Furthermore, consideration had to be given as to how it would operate throughout the school and who would be responsible for it. Staff and children thought about how the currency could be earned and the children were speedily introduced to the purpose of interest rates and how these would be determined. Moreover, consideration was also given as to what would happen if the currency was lost or stolen.

Establishing the Bank of Yeading

At the time of setting up the Bank of Yeading, Personal, Social, Health and Economic Education (PSHE), along with *Every Child Matters* (DfES, 2003), required enterprise and personal finance education to be taught in primary schools. The PSHE Association in 2009 stated:

> Education for economic wellbeing requires children and young people to learn how to manage their money on a day to day basis and to plan for a future where they can earn their own money through enterprise, as a worker or manager, either in the private or public sector. To be effective, education for economic wellbeing will follow the same principles as other aspects of PSHE. While the content and the kinds of experiences children may need to learn will vary, teaching and learning strategies will be similar. (PSHE 2009)

The principles behind the Bank of Yeading have indeed shown our children how to value what they have, work hard, contribute to the community and further develop life skills that are needed right across the curriculum as well as beyond school. The currency we established became known as 'Yeadoes' and the Yeado notes are in various denominations. A competition was held to produce a design for a Yeado note and the children decided on a design which has remained in circulation ever since. At the time of designing the Yeado, our Year 6 children were undertaking some maths work that involved examining exchange rates between countries as part of several activities relating to travel. This enabled the children to comprehend how monetary values were established and what they should consider when creating their own.

Much discussion took place around the skills required in the workplace, and the foundation for these skills was established with children in school. This Yeado system was regarded as part of the school's general reward system, and this system would link directly to school expectations. Therefore, the following set of criteria was chosen for earning Yeadoes:

- good attendance and punctuality
- excellent work
- updating reading record books
- bringing correct equipment to school, including PE kit
- handing in completed homework.

As in a real-life work context, bonuses can be earned; in school, children would be rewarded for handing homework in before the allocated time. Furthermore, it was agreed that a shop should be set up in which the children could spend their earnings.

At an early stage, a Yeado shop was set up so that goods could be purchased with the children's rewards. Some children automatically pooled their Yeadoes with other members of their own class. As this was a whole school initiative, teachers ensured that each child had an in-class Yeading Bank account set up on the school's system. They were also given a bank book to help them track their money flow. Children continue to have the opportunity to earn Yeadoes and spend these at the Yeado shop on goods or services. The kinds of goods that children can purchase include different types of stationery and some sports items, including footballs. The Bank of Yeading received recognition in our inspection report by the Office for Standards in Education as follows:

Attainment in mathematics has increased rapidly because pupils have an understanding of its practical application; in part due to the school's own banking system, 'Yeading Junior Bank'. Pupils earn 'Yeadoes' and bank them or spend them. Banking them earns interest. In the upper school, they are taught about loan sharks and how to avoid borrowing beyond one's means to repay the money. This is related back to their banking system, where 'Yeadoes' must be earned before they can be spent. Teachers selected children to manage the accounts within the class and linked the work directly with IT and Mathematics reinforcing life skills and curriculum skills. (Ofsted 2013)

The Bank of Yeading

The Bank of Yeading continues to be an integral part of the work in Financial Education. Volunteering and teamwork are two character virtues that are most apparent throughout the teaching and learning in this area. For example, in order to monitor and aggregate the Yeadoes, it became necessary to have a young team of volunteers throughout the school. Initially, each class teacher appointed a representative in class to calculate the Yeadoes gained by each child. These were then recorded on an Excel spreadsheet and children were able to have an update on their account as necessary.

In order to embed this further as a whole school system, bank director roles were established. As with other roles of responsibility within our school, children were encouraged to complete an application form expressing their interest in becoming a bank director. These were given to the Financial Education coordinator, who assessed the children on merit and ability to be resilient in the role. Guidance was given to the teaching team by the coordinator. From the beginning of the academic year 2017–2018, three different types of class bank manager roles were introduced: notably, an auditor, accounts manager and cash manager. Auditors check Yeadoes earned by each customer (child) by referring to the Yeadoes chart. Accounts managers record weekly Yeadoes on an Excel spreadsheet. Cash managers take Yeado deposits from customers or give earned Yeadoes to customers. Customers are looked after by managers and Yeadoes are banked. Each child has a physical bank book in which to record their Yeadoes. This gives children an opportunity to use their mathematical skills relating to money, such as calculating the balance on their account and working out the interest earned. All of these tasks directly relate to real-life skills and support the development of responsible learners with transferrable life skills. Through discussions with parents, it has also become apparent that the children would assist and guide them too.

Children showed great determination when following through the next stage of the career path that led them to apply to become a whole school bank director. Applicants for these prestigious positions were shortlisted by using 'Qualifications' and 'Experience' as success criteria for applications, and the successful applicants were then assessed using eligibility criteria. Children were able to request a character reference from their classroom teacher to support their application. 'Salary' and 'allowances' were also mentioned on the application form.

A more recent democratic approach has been put into effect, where children take ownership of the Bank of Yeading and each child has the opportunity to apply, and vote, for the new board of directors. A new board of directors was voted for directly by the pupils during the academic year 2018–2019.

Bank directors (children) are involved in the setting of whole school activities and help to explain those activities to members of staff and children, often during a whole school assembly. Directors are also involved with the training of classroom bank managers (e.g. using an Excel spreadsheet to record the flow of Yeadoes). Directors manage the Yeadoes shop and help to purchase goods for the shop by working on a budget set with the Financial Education coordinator. They then determine prices for goods and services. Finally, they record the total amount of Yeadoes spent during operating hours.

Understanding money

A significant number of activities have taken place over time which are related to enterprise or Financial Education and children have had plenty of opportunities to demonstrate their skills in this area. During 'My Money Week' in 2011, the school became part of a case study undertaken by pfeg, 'What Money Means', in relation to Yeading Junior School. The project taught parents and children the importance of managing personal finance. Furthermore, it demonstrated how to embed Financial Education into the school curriculum.

The objectives of the project were to provide children with opportunities to make personal choices regarding their money and also to provide children with experiences in order to gain an understanding of the value of money in real-life contexts. At that time, the school had a number of peer ambassadors who represented the school on various occasions. These ambassadors had the opportunity to make a presentation in central London in front of the Personal Finance Education Group. They shared experiences about being engaged in the programme 'What Money Means' and shared activities that had taken place to inspire children and adults on personal finance. These children also took part in a presentation in front of the Mayor of Hillingdon and finance officers from various departments in the local Civic Centre.

A further event called 'Spread the Word' aimed to share impacts with others and enabled the children to share their learning with around 40 schools from both primary and secondary contexts. The school was accredited with the Centre of Excellence status in 2011. As part of this project, the children undertook some growing activities in the school's polytunnel. These had a costing element which involved children estimating the cost of plants, amongst other things. In an article titled, 'Baby Economics', published in *The Spectator*, Clarissa Tan wrote:

> There's an excited buzz in the Year 6 class of Yeading Junior School, in outer London. The ten-year-olds recently set up a polytunnel in the school grounds, and now they're deciding which vegetables to plant in the new polythene greenhouse... In the UK, the main champion of financial education is a charity called the Personal Finance Education Group or pfeg. This is an outfit run from Shoreditch in London that helps schools plan and teach personal finance, often in a cross-curricular way (as part of maths, say, or so-called 'Personal Social Health & Economic' studies). Thanks partly to the organization's efforts, an All-Party Parliamentary Group on Financial Education for Young People was formed last year – with 226 cross-party MPs and peers, it's the largest such group in parliament. It's pfeg that's advising Yeading school, where the topic seems all the more crucial, seeing as children from disadvantaged backgrounds need all the financial acumen they can get. (Tan 2012)

Within a very short period of time, by 2013 our Key Stage 2 children had made significant strides in their knowledge, understanding and skills of Financial Education and Financial Literacy.

Children also wrote stories about money and shared ideas with each other. Other activities provided links to the Modern Foreign Languages

(MFL) curriculum. One particularly interesting decision was made with the children that involved setting up a 20 per cent discount in the Yeado shop if children spoke in French. Although this proved to be quite challenging, it was also extremely promotional in terms of developing further linguistic skills in a real-life, authentic context.

Many of the opportunities at the time led some children to have some really exciting experiences, such as meeting with the Chairman of British Airways, and visiting the Bank of England and Goldman Sachs. Some children also took part in enterprise projects linking directly with a local secondary school within the extended schools cluster. Children used the school's wider facilities to bake cakes and create plastic key rings, all of which were sold during Enterprise Week. Costing was explored; income was monitored; and the profit was assessed by the children involved.

In October 2013 a representative from one of the financial organizations to which the school had links visited Yeading Junior School and was extremely impressed with the children's knowledge and skills, noting in particular the work of our Year 3 children. The representative commented on the fact that money habits are formed at an early age. It was also encouraging to learn from a representative from another organization supporting us on our Financial Education journey that there was clear evidence of the teachers' passion in teaching and recognition of the important values being taught. The school was praised for its work in Financial Education. The management of money for children involves so much more in terms of personal development and links so well with our development of virtuous children.

Teachers at Yeading Junior School use the planning framework provided by Young Enterprise (2018) to both plan and assess Financial Education teaching and learning. As a junior school, our focus is on the following objectives:

- how to manage money
- becoming a critical consumer
- managing risks and emotions associated with money
- understanding the important role money plays in our lives.

Some of the work undertaken to cover these objectives involves using an online site provided by Young Enterprise called 'Cha Ching', which is a financial literacy programme. Other work is set up in conjunction with topics and themes as well as within Mathematics, and an example of this was the planning of a trip to Paris and using financial skills to work out the most cost-effective route. Other tasks included buying lunch in Paris and also working out the budget for the whole trip using exchange rates. This involved solving some complex mathematical problems, and the children needed to have a range of character virtues, too. Teamwork was very much at the fore, and various groups within the class were assigned a range of challenging activities. Determination was also in evidence, as the children needed to draw conclusions and answer questions connected to a trip that they eventually undertook. The school has since also engaged with enterprise programmes in conjunction with the Mayor's Fund for London and has also been part of a pilot scheme involving enterprise advisers coming into the school (London Enterprise Adviser Network 2016).

Recognizing innovative practice and deepening understanding

In 2013, the school was introduced to a project launched by the Illegal Money Lending Team (IMLT). Increasing concern had been raised about the financial dilemmas of families and the practice of loan sharks trying to encourage parents to borrow beyond their means. The IMLT was introduced to the school by the Personal Finance Education Group, and because of the children's great understanding of money issues at a primary level, we were requested to test out some new materials. The school trialled lessons with Year 6 pupils which were designed to raise further awareness and develop greater knowledge about the illegal practices of loan sharks.

In February 2014, *BBC News* filmed at Yeading Junior School and focused on loan sharks. Children were fascinated to learn that the educational resources they were using had been funded by the money confiscated from loan sharks' illegal practices. They felt this was a very moral and appropriate way to use the funding. The filming undertaken related to the lessons that the school had been trialling around the dangers of loan sharks. The children were engaged in exploring moral issues and dilemmas around the dangers of loan sharks and maturely understood the impact. In March 2014, BBC's *Newsround* also filmed at Yeading Junior School. In one classroom, when a child was asked what a loan shark was, they replied that 'a loan shark is an illegal money lender who is friendly to you but then after a while they turn nasty and put interest on the money they lent out' (Codd 2014).

Work was not only undertaken with the children but with parents as well in the Community House. The IMLT and the Money Advice Service worked with parents and offered advice around money management and debt. Children were advised to talk to parents about their learning, and information was also provided from school.

Our Community Education Award, in 2014, was testament to the work that goes on beyond the classroom within the Community House and out in the wider community. The Community Education Awards are an annual celebration and recognition of schools' efforts to help children and young people become responsible community members. Yeading Junior School won the 'Personal Money Management Award 2014' and with this achievement was recognized for a Community Education Award (Community Education Awards 2014).

An article that was featured in the London Borough of Hillingdon (2014) newspaper reports: 'YEADING Junior School in Hayes is celebrating after winning a national award for a project all about money management. They were crowned winners of the Personal Money Management Award in the Community Education Awards 2014. The awards are organized by the Police Community Clubs of Great Britain and aim to reward schools that have gone above and beyond promoting positive citizenship and responsible decision-making.' A presentation ceremony was held in the hall of Yeading Junior School with representatives from the Personal Finance Education Group, Metro Bank, Corporate Communication from the London Borough of Hillingdon and Mark Luton, Chief Inspector of Hillingdon.

We were delighted to have been featured in *The Telegraph* for our work on personal finance. The children proved to be so knowledgeable when speaking to the news reporter and were delighted to know that their work would be featured in a national paper, thereby making a difference to other learners. Jessica Winch from *The Telegraph* set the scene in the Year 6 classroom at Yeading Junior School and outlined the importance of learning to manage and understand money:

> On a grey Thursday morning in west London, a class of 10-year-olds are converting the cost of a café crème into sterling. Next, they work out how much it would cost to take the class with five adults to Paris on a school trip, comparing various transport options and special offers. Underneath a colourful punctuation pyramid and pictures of equilateral and scalene triangles, the children tap away on calculators, discussing the price of petrol and the benefit of a group discount. The children,

pupils at Yeading Junior School in Hayes, west London, are learning the basics of personal finance. (Winch 2013)

She goes on to discuss government changes that have been outlined in relation to the 2013 new National Curriculum:

> Last week saw the publication of the new draft National Curriculum for England, which includes financial education in maths and 'citizenship'. Personal finance is already taught in schools in Wales, Scotland and Northern Ireland. Following a public consultation, the final version of the new curriculum will be presented to schools this September and introduced in classrooms next year. Citizenship education, which is proposed from Year 7, includes lessons in UK law and governance as well as teaching children how to manage their money. (Winch 2013)

Despite the subject being non-compulsory, our school continues to teach and embed the learning within the curriculum.

Entrepreneurship

The school has developed links with such financial institutions as Metro Bank, whose representatives provide 'Money Zone' sessions for our children. They describe the programme as follows: 'Our financial education programme teaches primary school kids how money, banking and personal finance works' (Metro Bank 2018). Therefore, Metro Bank managers come to Yeading Junior School to teach children practical Financial Education lessons. We have built a strong link with Metro Bank and this relates directly to our Centre of Excellence status. As an example, during February 2018, children whose classes were engaged in the Financial Education programme delivered by Metro Bank received an activity book and one grape. The children were given the grape as a means of explaining interest. If children managed to go through the whole session without eating their grape, they would receive a second grape by way of interest. It was reported that the children found the task quite challenging and many received no interest as a result! Class teachers, however, provided positive feedback to the Financial Education coordinator about these lessons.

In July 2017, John McDonnell, Shadow Chancellor of the Exchequer and Member of Parliament for Hayes and Harlington, was invited to Yeading

Junior School to speak with our bank's board of directors and also the other children in assembly. The purpose of the visit was to enable the children to learn about the importance of Financial Education practically, both nationally and internationally. Mr McDonnell discussed real-life financial issues with our children, including the different types of banks and borrowing. Following discussions with the board of directors, he identified that the Bank of Yeading is a bank that gets in money and gives out money to its customers. Other banks can focus on speculative stock and could risk losing vast amounts of money. He advised our bank directors to avoid over-extending when borrowing and recommended to the children that they carry out an annual review and get feedback from other children.

The board of directors were determined to act upon the advice given by Mr McDonnell, and they worked with the Financial Education coordinator to prepare an annual review for the Bank of Yeading. Each class completed a grid to show the total amount of Yeadoes earned by the entire class, the most Yeadoes earned by one pupil and the most interest earned by one pupil for saving Yeadoes in their bank account. An assembly was then held, and all findings were shared with the school. The top earners and savers were awarded certificates. Children had the opportunity to also calculate total spending at the Yeado shop by calculating the total number of each note (i.e. 1Y, 2Y, 5Y, 10Y and 20Y) received from customers during shop opening hours. A great number of skills were involved in this process, including mathematical, literacy and social skills, as well as many identifiable virtues. Honesty and integrity have often been explored through all aspects of financial literacy with bank directors, as well as with other children. This area has given rise to many moral discussions and debates, not least about money lending. As a result of the work relating to illegal money lending, a number of children visited the House of Lords through the kind invitation of Lord Toby Harris, who had visited the school and was impressed with the children's monetary understanding and concerns.

Another exciting and more recent endeavour for the school has been engaging with the Peter Jones Foundation and the programme entitled 'Tycoon Enterprise Competition'. We entered this competition in both Autumn 2018 and Autumn 2017 (when it was known as 'Tycoon in Schools'), and a Year 3 child made a profit ratio of 261 per cent during the trading phase (October–December 2017). He was determined to use a loan to earn a profit and ensured that the cost of sales was kept to a minimum by using a business plan. The boy created a product called

'Perfect Pancakes'. His business plan described the product. Start-up costs were very accurately calculated and included unit costs, quantities and total costs of all the ingredients required to make pancakes. Discounts were also available for bulk purchase of this product. He created his own unique logo and advertisement. A selling price was set and, based on estimated pancakes sold, a total forecasted profit was made. Segments of this plan, along with other children's plans involved in the competition, were put on display and shared with children at Yeading Junior School. This display was a problem-solving display and linked to Mathematics. After the trading period, actual costs of sales and actual profits were compared with forecasted amounts. Children found this very interesting and were amazed by the results.

In October 2018, our children entered the 'Tycoon Enterprise' (formerly 'Tycoon in Schools') competition as part of their Financial Education learning. This national enterprise competition, launched by Peter Jones CBE for students aged 6–18, aims to encourage entrepreneurship in the UK. Children create innovative business plans to try and secure a start-up loan to cover the costs of their sales. There are four stages of the competition: business plan, trading, evaluation and results.

As a home learning activity, all children had the opportunity to complete a business plan using the template provided by Tycoon Enterprise. Four businesses were then selected to compete in the competition from the many applications, following the successful submission of accurate business plans. These businesses formed themselves with roles and responsibilities decided upon and agreed by all members. The four businesses were named: 'Awesome Origami', 'Cupcake Delight', 'Daiisy' and 'Cool Beads'.

Trading was successful overall, and the children learned from the reality of owning and managing a business. Children in businesses continually reviewed their business strategies and products, some creating new items as part of their sales stock (e.g. new origami creations). Some businesses focused on how to reduce the cost of sales in order to maximize profit (e.g. recycled wrapping paper used as a resource to create a bookmark and some of the origami designs, such as the petals of a tulip). Product modifications took place and the 'Awesome Origami' business also hired additional staff (other children) to help with their production of origami products.

Some businesses focused on marketing strategies and how best to attract customers through price reductions, discounts offered (e.g. Awesome Origami offered a 10 per cent discount for first-time buyers), attractive descriptions (e.g. Cool Beads came up with 'Unique personalized treasures handmade with love!') and slogans (e.g. Cupcake Delight's, 'Take a break, have a cupcake' and Cool Beads', 'Once they're gone, they're gone!'). Trading lasted for less than two weeks, which was a slight deviation from the official trading period. However, this time frame worked out well at our school. It took place both inside and outside the school, dependent upon each business strategy. Money was banked daily by the Financial Education coordinator and amounts were entered into the Tycoon Enterprise Competition dashboard and a graph tracking the trading of each business was generated.

The results of profit and return on investment for each business venture at Yeading Junior School are shown in Table 7.1 and our top-performing business team 'Awesome Origami' was placed 16th nationally.[1] Evaluations were carried out and children reflected on both business successes and failures in a positive manner (e.g. describing how to become a more efficient business in the future). Thus, as Jones states, 'What enterprise and entrepreneurship does is show that there is no such thing as failure, there's only feedback. I think that's a really important message to tell every child' (Gurney-Read 2015).

Table 7.1 Results for profit and return on investment for each business venture

Business Name	Profit	Return on Investment
Awesome Origami	£93.10	4,655%
Daiisy	£69.57	117.92%
Cool Beads	£49.85	73.31%
Cupcake Delight	-£9.56	-19.29%

By way of reflection it is interesting to note that this area of learning has been sustained for over ten years and it still continues to grow and develop. There are some interesting elements that have given Financial Literacy longevity, which include the full engagement of the headteacher and governors, as well as all other staff and children. Having different members of staff coordinate the area over time, preferring new ideas, has

---

1   In 2019, five business teams entered the competition (including our original Awesome Origami team) and, in relation to profits, our Yeading Junior School top-performing business team called BK Charms was placed 2nd nationally – interestingly, Awesome Origami, our third performing team this time around was placed 4th nationally. Truly remarkable accomplishments.

ensured that different experiences and opportunities are always available. Teamwork has certainly been evidenced and there have been numerous opportunities to volunteer. Furthermore, through the school's social action activities, the children have raised significant funds for charity. Children have also planned and prepared budgets when undertaking social action projects. An example of this would be the WE 'Walk for Water' campaign in April 2018, where children walked to Brunel University London to raise money for clean water and were able to work out, through their fantastic efforts, that they had managed to generate sufficient funds to give 69 people clean water for life.

'WE Are Rafikis' was another WE Schools learning experience and money-raising event for children at Yeading Junior School that sparked their passion for volunteering. Advertisements were created at our school and children acted as salespersons. Each bracelet was handmade in Africa and money earned from each Rafiki purchased made an impact in three ways: it helped the artisan who made it earn a living and save for the future; it provided clean water or school supplies to a member of a developing community; and it allowed children to fundraise for a cause they cared about. Children learned about these causes through visitors from WE Schools coming to our school and showing video clips from the WE Schools' website, as well as through their Financial Education lessons. The children were determined to make a change and support people less well-off internationally. Children demonstrated compassion to people in different circumstances.

The examples included within this chapter illuminate some of the ways in which we have worked with a range of businesses and national/international organizations to transform Yeading Junior School into a Centre of Excellence that successfully delivers practical and sustainable Financial Education. This has incorporated the creation of engaging and inspiring learning programmes, alongside staff development and training. As articulated by Young Money:

> Young people are at the heart of the programme. The goal is that they leave school with the knowledge, skills and confidence to be able to make informed and independent financial decisions. (Young Money 2018)

The Jubilee Centre for Character and Virtues in their *Framework for Character Education in Schools* (2017, p.8) state: 'Schools need to provide opportunities for children to exercise the virtues in practice as well as encourage a rich discourse of virtue language, understanding and reasoning.' The many and varied opportunities provided at Yeading Junior School enable children to be virtuous and demonstrate the application of character virtues in real-life contexts. Financial Literacy is most certainly an area that has made this goal possible.

References

Codd, D. (2014) 'The dangers of loan sharks to be taught in schools.' *BBC News*, 3 March. Accessed at 07/05/2019 at www.bbc.co.uk/news/business-26376737

Community Education Awards (2014) *Personal Money Management Award*. Accessed 25/05/19 at www.communityeducationawards.co.uk/our-winners/personal-money-management-award

Department for Education and Skills (DfES) (2003) *Every Child Matters*. Green Paper. London: DfES.

Gurney-Read, J. (2015) 'Peter Jones: "The government needs to wake up; we need proper business education in schools."' *The Telegraph*, 13 March. Accessed 24/05/19 at www.telegraph.co.uk/education/educationopinion/11470341/Peter-Jones-the-Government-needs-to-wake-up-we-need-proper-business-education-in-schools.html

Illegal Money Lending Team (2013) *Stop Loan Sharks*. Accessed 25/05/19 at www.ssaspb.org.uk/Professionals/Illegal-Money-Lending-Team-information.pdf

Jubilee Centre for Character and Virtues (2017) *A Framework for Character Education in Schools*. Birmingham: The Jubilee Centre for Character and Virtues (University of Birmingham).

Hillingdon & Uxbridge Times (2014) 'Award for Hayes school where money really DOES matter', 23 July, 2014. 'Council congratulates pupils on national award.' July. Accessed 25/05/18 at www.hillingdontimes.co.uk/news/11360207.award-for-hayes-school-where-money-really-does-matter

London Enterprise Adviser Network (2016) *Primary School Handbook*. Mayor's Fund for London and Team London. Accessed 25/05/10 at www.london.gov.uk/sites/default/files/ean_primary_school_guide.pdf

Metro Bank (2018) *Money Zone*. Accessed 25/05/19 at www.metrobankonline.co.uk/about-us/kids-zone

Office for Standards in Education (Ofsted) (2013) *Inspection Report: Yeading Junior School, 23–24 October*. Manchester: Crown. Accessed 20/05/19 at https://files.api.ofsted.gov.uk/v1/file/2289289

Personal, Social, Health and Economic (PSHE) Association (2009) *Programme of Study: Economic Wellbeing and Financial Capability*. Accessed 20/05/18 at www.pshe-association.org.uk/curriculum-and-resources/curriculum

Tan, C. (2012) 'Baby economics: How – and why – ten-year-olds are being taught to run a business.' *The Spectator*, 24 March. Accessed 03/05/2019 at www.spectator.co.uk/2012/03/baby-economics

Tycoon Enterprise Competition (2018). Accessed 05/10/19 at www.tycoon.com

Tycoon in Schools (2017). Accessed 25/05/10 at www.tycoon.com

WE Schools. Accessed 25/04/19 at www.we.org

Winch, J. (2013) 'First steps on the finance footpath.' *The Telegraph*, 10 February. Accessed 25/05/10 at www.telegraph.co.uk/finance/personalfinance/9858644/First-steps-on-the-finance-footpath.html

Young Enterprise & Young Money (2018) *Financial Education: Centres of Excellence*. Accessed 25/05/10 at www.young-enterprise.org.uk/teachers-hub/financial-education/financial-education-programmes/centres-of-excellence

Young Money (2018) *A Step by Step Guide to Achieving a Centre of Excellence Award in Financial Education.* London: Young Enterprise. Accessed 25/05/19 at www.young-enterprise.org.uk/wp-content/uploads/2019/01/CoE-Step-by-Step-Guide-2018-YM_FE-v15_.pdf

Chapter 8

Engendering Pride and the Road to Achievement

CAROLE JONES

The *Road to Achievement* is a phrase and image emblazoned on every classroom door at Yeading Junior School. It conveys a sense of unity and common desire to attain success step by step. It is not incidental that the road curves and leads into the distance; however, the road remains on a continuum.

This chapter outlines the impact of character education on the school, individuals therein and the wider community, by showcasing our 'Voice Box', embedding social action and demonstrating that success leads to further success.

The Voice Box

One key outcome from the introduction of character education in the school has been the strength of pupil voice across all aspects of school life and beyond. We are proud of the confidence with which children articulate views and opinions and are able to engage in healthy debate with their peers. At one point in the life of the school we had a pupil forum of representatives across the school to discuss in-school issues. The membership initially included one child from each class, often nominated by a teacher.

Yeading Junior School has many avenues and opportunities for enabling children's voices to be heard. Beyond our 'Agents of Change' the school also has what is known as the 'Voice Box', which is a collective of elected children – two representatives from each class chosen by the other children

– who discuss school and external issues as well as input into the School Improvement Plan. Discussions that take place are then shared with their own class members.

The Voice Box is defined by the children at Yeading Junior School as:

- helping the school to make improvements and changes
- children having rights to express themselves and be heard
- ensuring that all children are listened to.

Furthermore, the children have stated:

Children should be involved in policy writing so they can actually understand the policy and have a voice.

In their publication entitled *Listening to and Involving Children and Young People*, the Department for Education (DfE 2014) writes that the government is committed to the promotion and protection of children's rights, in line with the United Nations Convention on the Rights of the Child. It believes that children and young people should have opportunities to express their opinion in matters that affect their lives.

The publication goes on to discuss ways in which children can contribute to decision making using their democratic rights. It talks about ways in which children develop responsibility and refers to how increasing confidence impacts on academic skills and promotes good attainment.

At Yeading Junior School, we encourage our children to take part in participative work across the school. Through discussions and questions with guest speakers at the meetings with the Voice Box, children have debated issues or reflected on current thinking.

The further development of oratory skills has led to significant improvements in writing. Prolific letter writing is very much part of the culture of the school. Children write letters to request the opportunity to take part in a range of activities or indeed to lead on one of these many activities, as well as outlining their skills within 'job' applications for different leadership roles. They may also put forward the idea of running a club for their peers or engaging in a charitable project, as the following excerpt, written by a small group of Year 5 pupils, exemplifies:

▓ The reason why we would like to volunteer to run a lunchtime club is to be able to work with the Year 3/4 children to help boost their confidence in performing dance and drama. We want other children to have good self-esteem and believe in themselves.

Through the development of social action and character education, speaking skills have been transformed. Whereas in the past children may have been reticent to articulate their views in public arenas or have shown a need for prompt sheets or cue cards, their resilience now shines through. They are recognized as articulate, proud and enthusiastic speakers who have been called upon to speak in front of charity groups and companies who fund these charitable organizations. Children have had such incredible opportunities, for which they feel justly proud.

Two such wonderful experiences relate to WE Schools events where, on two separate special occasions, two different children spoke to a prestigious audience. Both children spoke with confidence and prowess. One very quiet child even spoke about social action with skill and confidence at the Wembley Arena in front of an audience in excess of 12,000 people (see Chapter 4). The depth of the character virtues in school meant that other children showed great pride in the achievement of their peers. The sense of pride acts as a motivational force. Children have become such confident speakers both in class and whole school contexts. They speak enthusiastically without recourse to prompts. Teachers, parents and the community are very proud of these life-long skills. As a result of this nurtured ability, the school is frequently asked to select children to speak in a range of forums, bringing joy, pride and inspiration to the community.

Bringing in skilled speakers from outside the school has had a profound effect on the learners, and they in turn emulate what they see. At a recent event a number of our 'Special Agents' were captivated by the interesting journey the motivational speaker had taken prior to being successful in his role. He talked about the adversity of suddenly becoming incapacitated by a serious illness and how having the confidence to be able to discuss this in a range of arenas led him to understand that he was empowered to both motivate himself and others to overcome difficulties.

Through the weaving of character education throughout school life, there has grown an intrinsic understanding amongst the children that they can all use effective strategies to speak up and have their voices heard. This is clearly evident in assemblies, during which both younger and older children willingly volunteer opinions and answers and it has become customary for children of all ages to deliver clear messages to the rest of the school without prior notification or rehearsal. An example of this is when the *Cable News Network* (*CNN*) visited Yeading Junior School in association with WE Schools. A Year 4 child had the confidence to state that her view of freedom is like when a bird is released from a cage where it has been confined. This child was unabashed about the cameras facing her and just spoke with confidence, even reframing her response when it had been misheard.

The school has enjoyed taking part in a number of successful activities where children have demonstrated they are empowered and confident. These include working with Children's Writers and Illustrators for Stories and Literacy (CWISL) and their 'Shout West' writing project for schools in West London, 'Shakespeare for Schools' and the 'Young Ambassadors – City Pitch'. City Pitch is a platform for children to pitch for money from the Mayor of London's Fund for a well-thought-out and carefully budgeted project. The children's most recent attempt to do this was in respect of seeking funds to support some work they hope to undertake in the school's Community House.[1]

The funds the children pitched for were to be used for further development and expansion of the school's intergenerational work. The whole idea for this particular project was instigated by the children. Having previously reflected on the success and positive outcomes of their intergenerational work with the MHA Northwood Live at Home Scheme (as detailed in Chapter 5), the children wished to engage with their own older people and introduce them to the older people in Northwood.

Young Ambassadors – City Pitch

Six children from Years 5 and 6 all actively engaged as a group on their pitch for funds. They agreed that they had to capture the audience from the outset and so decided to begin the pitch by greeting everyone in a variety of languages. Individuals within the group took turns in speaking the lines they had previously put together themselves. They worked cohesively as a group on the day and whilst preparing for the pitch, and were extremely confident.

---

1   A former caretaker's house that is used for the benefit of the school's local community. It is a place of friendship, training and personal development that is referred to throughout this book.

Their speech was as follows:

We are from Yeading Junior School and have come here today to pitch for £1,000 to fund our Intergenerational Programme.

This programme started two years ago with a handful of Year 5 children going to the Northwood Live at Home Scheme to work with the elderly and teach them how to use an iPad. As you know, technology is extremely important in this day and age.

Technology has become the means of communication.

Before we started our work with the elderly, they had no idea how to use an iPad! This may come as a surprise to you, but it's true. We are extremely proud to say that the elderly now know how to use the internet, shop online and even FaceTime their loved ones across the seven seas!

We have made some extremely good friends, like S and J, who are always so excited to see us.

Our work with the elderly has just begun and we would like to take our intergenerational programme to the next level. Building on the relationships we have, we will use the funds to run coffee mornings and workshops in our Community House. The workshops will give the elderly the opportunity to go out and explore a different place. It will give them motivation to come out of their comfort zone and meet new people and eliminate aspects of loneliness. We aim to start our workshops in the New Year – February 2019 to be precise!

We will do some arts and crafts activities, like making cards, embroidery, and even painting with them, along with playing board games and having interesting discussions. We want to provide the elderly with a safe place where they can integrate freely and speak about their past. The stories of the olden days can be shared.

The workshops will be led by the Special Agents, who will, under the direction of the adults, help set up the Community House and serve refreshments to the elderly. I'm sure a cup of tea and cake will go a long way. Cake is usually their favourite food to eat!

At the end of the workshops we would like to throw a summer party for them. Many of them have probably not attended a party for a long time. We will have lunch and games and the elderly will have the opportunity to see some performances by our children. We have lots of musical instruments, and children at Yeading are always looking for an audience.

The summer party will also be a celebration of the dedicated inter-generational work we have been doing for the past two years.

Now, you're probably thinking £1,000 is a lot of money to run workshops and do a summer party, but we also need support with the iPad training if we want it to be sustainable.

At the moment it costs us £65 a week to take the children to the elderly home. If we could have some support with this, it would be great. We all know what school budgets are like! No one's ever got any money!

Please find on your tables the budget for our project and we promise not to waste any of your money. This project will involve the local community, as we will invite grandparents from the school. It will be lovely to hear stories from this vibrantly diverse community that we live in.

Before we finish, we would like to share some photographs of our work with the elderly so far! These photographs show that we work in cohesion with the local community and we plan to carry on the amazing work throughout years to come.

In these photographs you can see us working with the elderly and the elderly transferring their skills to the children. They are showing our children how to knit, an art which has slowly disappeared. We put a show on for them last Christmas called 'Cinderella-Rockafella'. They had a really enjoyable afternoon.

The children finished by thanking everyone for listening and they said thank you in different languages.

The bid was successful, and it was with great pride that the children embarked on their project and reflected on the outcomes of their work. The great sense of ownership of a project, the cascading to others and drawing out identifiable virtues becomes a great motivator for children who have seen other projects flourish into greater things. The whole notion of working across geographic areas in their own borough facilitates the children's understanding that projects can be replicated, not only to assist others but also to have an impact on one's own extended family. As one Year 5 child stated, 'Intergenerational work has helped me to understand my grandparents more and develop patience.' Sharing their thoughts and ideas with younger members of their families or school community also assists others in growing the virtues.

Our goal in promoting social action most certainly has resonance with the work of Dr Marilyn Price-Mitchell, who states:

Character education in the early years helps build strengths like honesty, responsibility, fairness and compassion – internal assets that lead to happiness and well-being. These are the kinds of human qualities that foster *responsible citizens*, children who grow up to donate to food drives, recycle their trash, or help during a crisis. (Price-Mitchell 2015)

Embedding social action

The school is extremely proud of the successful embedding of social action within and beyond the curriculum, extending its reach to local projects as well as global work. For us, social action has been a compelling journey linking intricately with our character virtues to the point where it is second nature for the children to act.

Peter Mountstephen, Chair of National Primary Heads, quoted in *Scoping a Quality Framework for Youth Social Action*, states that:

> Through youth social action our pupils develop the confidence and resilience to succeed with their school work but also a sense that they can have a hugely positive impact on others in their community. They develop attitudes and behaviours that help them to flourish in the classroom and go on to succeed in work and life. They really are the young citizens we all want to see in our communities. (Young Foundation 2013)

Previous chapters have referred to the school's engagement in social action which is wholly embedded in the life of the school. Children and staff have worked enthusiastically to collect goods and raise funds for charity. The 'Bake Sales' have formed part of the WE School campaigns; the latest of which generated £600 for charity. The fact that the school has developed a strong moral compass was indicated the day before the Bake Sale, when it became very evident that few cakes had been brought in for sale. A timely reminder from our 'Agents' reflecting on the character virtues yielded great success. Not only did families generously donate cakes, they also sent money in for children to purchase cakes. The school features in the *WE Schools Global Workbook* of educational resources for this aspect of social action on a previous occasion. When reflecting upon what inspired them to get involved with Free the Children, one year 6 child states, 'There's so many children out there who don't have the privileges that we have. What made me want to raise money for Free the Children was that it's so good to help other children and get them opportunities as well' (WE Schools Global Workbook 2015–2016: 55).

A recent project involved children contributing to survival packs for the homeless. Many items were brought in by children and their families to include in the packs, which were put together by the DePaul Trust. The knowledge and sensitivity shown by the children during an assembly about the homeless is indicative of the interest and pride families take in the community around them. One child said that his father spoke to homeless people using their names in the knowledge that one should always grant dignity to others.

Children are immensely proud of the learners in their own classes and are always ready to give due praise as necessary. Some of the older children have worked in their own break times, unprompted, with children newly arrived in the country. Usually this has been around 'teaching' new vocabulary or reading together.

Pride in learning is at the fore within our families. Projects that have been an extension of a class activity have been developed further at home through a variety of media. Carefully crafted models and booklets frequently appear in school. We have had parents who worked in school using their arts and crafts skills to lift learning and support the acquisition of new skills. They demonstrated many of our virtues and excellent volunteering skills; one example of this was captured during a celebration of the work children had undertaken to support sustainability in another country: a parent made life-size models of goats as an addition to a display. The children had raised money through various acts of social action to fund the purchase of goats overseas to help families to be self-sustaining. The addition of these goats to the display also helped to enhance the younger children's understanding of how the cycle of sustainability worked. Furthermore, a group of parents from the Community House undertook their own fundraising activity, selling refreshments in the front garden of the Community House to add to the money raised by the children. This was a perfect example of the children and families uniting together in social action. As stated within *A Framework for Character Education in Schools*:

> The ultimate aim of character education is not only to make individuals better persons but to create the social and institutional conditions within which all human beings can flourish. Social and institutional conditions of this kind require that all members of the society contribute in ways that collectively provide everyone with opportunities to live well. Conversely, the cultivation of individual character is most likely to succeed in exactly such conditions of

reciprocity and equal opportunity. Fundamental to these conditions is an ethos of cooperation and mutual goodwill. (Jubilee Centre 2017, p.2)

Pride and motivation

A discussion paper from the Cabinet Office (2015, p.5) outlined that 'social action is about people coming together to help improve their lives and solve the problems that are important in their communities'.

Each day, children are reminded about the ten virtues that the school hold to be of great importance. Over time, with staff and children alike, it has become evident that the virtues do not operate in isolation but work intrinsically together. Each teacher develops this within their own classroom, through their own practice and modelling. The adults demonstrate pride in the work of their school and community, which in turn affects and promotes change amongst the children. Success leads to further success and our children really understand this.

For example, when it came to entering a local singing competition, it was decided to enter with a choir of children who wanted to sing as opposed to a carefully honed choir; in fact, it was an extremely aspirational class and their talented music coordinator teacher who took on the challenge. Never having taken part in such a competition before, both staff and children were delighted to have come first in all three categories within their group. This spurred the school, staff and children on to achieve further success the following year. Success promotes success and determination comes to the fore.

Whole school assemblies and class assemblies performed in front of parents always refer to our character virtues and are often themed to that effect. There is a constant sharing of what the virtues signify and how they are linked. The virtues are emblazoned on the wall surrounding the school logo in the hall and act as a visual and constant reminder of our school philosophy. Pride in performance is demonstrated through drama, music and dance, where children perform to a high standard. The confidence gained through taking part in a range of innovative activities in front of a wide-ranging audience has given children the ability to speak, dance and sing with great skill.

At a recent Christmas production, it was impressive to observe so many children undertaking solo roles, really rising to the occasion. At this time the school also pledged to help the Foundation for Social Change and Inclusion (FSCI) 'Christmas Box Appeal' (2018) to spread some happiness and also support families in Bulgaria. As this is a costly period for families and a time when other charitable causes are being supported, the school pledged to put together 100 boxes full of goods for many vulnerable children and families in refugee camps. The children knew that this would be a challenge; however, driven by our young Special Agents, the school took pride in filling one 145 decorated boxes. These boxes were collected for shipment to southeast Europe to be distributed by the charity there.

At this time, as previously mentioned in Chapter 4, the children had undertaken a homelessness campaign in the local area. Many items were brought into school to be distributed by a local charity. Inspired by our young leaders of this campaign, a number of teaching and non-teaching staff have trained as volunteers at a nearby winter soup kitchen run by the same charity. It leads to the question: Who inspires who?

The compassion and respect shown by both our young and older volunteers has been motivational for others, causing a ripple effect throughout the community. It has also had a positive effect on our own families, a number of whom have, on occasion, found themselves in this vulnerable situation. An emergency provision box for this local charity remains in the school entrance way. Year 6 children have said:

> I have learned that there are many homeless people. I have always wanted to help them and understand how to do this safely. There could be families in our own community we could help with our emergency box. Giving to others makes me feel happy because I feel that I have made a difference and it has a ripple effect.

> The emergency box has helped in many ways, if anyone has something spare to help our community, they can put it in our collection box. I have learned that there are people in our community that need support and we are fortunate. If we have the power to help, then we should. I have a positive outlook and when I do things to help others, it encourages me to do more. Your actions can be infectious. An example of this would be as Special Agents if we do something the whole school is sure to do that too.

Over time, the school has engaged with a range of partners, as is reflected in previous chapters of this book. It was with great pride that a small group of children were invited to speak about their recent social action at #iwill ('Step Up to Serve'). The children engaged fully in the event and talked in an interested manner throughout; they spoke well and confidently; they demonstrated great dignity and fantastic teamwork. Their presentation caught the attention of others in the field of character education and has enabled the school to network further.

An 'Exceptional Agent' card was given to identified children when teachers recognized that these children had consistently demonstrated the virtues in formal learning, as well as during informal situations in school. Often those identified demonstrated all of the virtues strongly through learning and attitudes to the wider aspects of the curriculum. These children were subsequently awarded a headteacher's certificate in recognition of their achievements. Internal awards are also given on other occasions, and more recently these have all had a character focus. The children's writing frequently reflects on this character learning. As mentioned earlier, the children at Yeading Junior School have become prolific letter writers over time. Numerous letters have been written by them, either focusing on volunteering or stating how important the virtues have become to their everyday life within and outside school. On numerous occasions the children think deeply about the themes shared in assemblies and draw on their knowledge of character virtues. As one Year 5 child stated, 'if you do not show curiosity you do not make progress'. Children are encouraged to reflect upon and write about ways in which character virtues can make a positive change both within and outside school.

The following excerpt is from a letter of application, written by a Year 6 child, to be considered for the role of Special Agent of Change.

> Ever since I went to school I've always been very coy, like everyone in my class says, well...not everyone I guess. However, when I got to know and learn more about the Character Virtues I have been showing a lot of progress with my confidence and I am now a confident speaker.
>
> I cannot believe I am at the top of the school so quickly. It's just phenomenal! Now that I've reached to the highest year of the school I will be an amazing role model for the younger pupils. I've been using the Character Virtues within my everyday life in and out of school, it truly makes me a better person. I will always represent this school with all of my pride and dignity wherever I am.
>
> A few ways that I show the Character Virtues are, for example, when someone sitting near me is struggling on something, I go and help them, which is showing an act of kindness and teamwork. Another way that I represent the Character Virtues is by showing respect to everyone around me no matter who they are.

I always reflect back on my work to see if I spot any mistakes (which I do) but that way I learn more. I would like to say more ways that I show the Character Virtues but then this letter will be so long and I'm not the only one writing a letter that's for sure.

I really hope I become a Special Agent of Change.

Yours sincerely

All of our agents like to be identified and will proudly talk of their work, whether they are Special Agents (leaders) or Agents (leaders in waiting). Wearing badges to represent children's leadership within the school has had a positive effect on all children. As a result of this we purchased Agent badges for all children. The children display a sense of pride in following the virtues and in identifying them throughout all aspects of school life. This becomes particularly evident when visitors come into school. One particular occasion (30 October 2018) when this was shown was on a visit to Yeading Junior School by Dame Julia Cleverdon on behalf of #iwill ('Step Up to Serve'). The #iwill campaign is a UK-wide initiative that promotes practical action in the service of others. It aims to:

> make social action part of life for as many 10- to 20-year-olds as possible by the year 2020. *Step Up to Serve* is the charity that coordinates the collective effort of the #iwill campaign by connecting campaign partners, communicating the stories and impact of quality social action and challenging partners to do more. The Patron of *Step Up to Serve* and the #iwill campaign is HRH The Prince of Wales and it is governed by an independent board as well as having cross-party support. Ultimately, the purpose is to have all young people given the chance to take part in meaningful social action – building a habit for life and further empowering them to be more active citizens today and in the future. (Step Up to Serve n.d.)

The #iwill campaign was formed in 2013, following a set of recommendations made by Dame Julia Cleverdon DCVO CBE and Amanda Jordan OBE to the prime minister concerning how to increase the quality and quantity of youth social action. Barriers identified at the time included:

> a shortage of activities in education from 10 upwards; confusion in the education and business sectors about the kind of initiatives they could support; failure to promote and inspire young people to take part; and

an absence of a coherent vision to promote a culture of youth social action. (#iwill n.d.)

The recommendations were to:

> create an easy to navigate 'service journey' for young people; scale up programmes to fill gaps in provision; embed social action in young people's educational experience (school, further and higher education); develop a culture of promoting and celebrating youth social action comparable to effective programmes run in other countries around the world. (#iwill n.d.)

Yeading Junior School has engaged in the #iwill campaign since 2013.[2] We have recently been selected by this charitable organization to take part in the Primary Ambassador Pilot Programme focusing on young people taking social action to improve society and the world they live in. Dame Julia was joined by the Deputy CEO of Step Up to Serve. Our children performed an assembly showcasing an array of projects that we have undertaken. Our homeless campaign, the most recent project, was rated highly by Dame Julia. She wrote a wonderful letter to the children, following her visit to our school, congratulating them on their excellent efforts as shown below:

> We were impressed to learn of the impact your social action and volunteering has had both for your local community and for others in distant countries. We loved your singing, dancing and the play that was so brilliantly acted to help us see how you are embedding social action and volunteering in subjects like geography, mathematics, English, science and art. We will be using the video of your performance to help us spread the work to other schools. As Primary Ambassadors for the #iwill campaign, you shine a beacon that lights the way for others. (Cleverdon 2018)

Children themselves have identified the tremendous differences that whole teams can make. They take great pride in working together to effect change. The words of the children below give a flavour of the impact of their journeys thus far:

---

2   www.iwill.org.uk/pledge/yeading-junior-school

Year 5 male

◼ It improves our academic achievements as we work together and help each other in the classroom.

Year 6 male

◼ Character education stays with us at school and family life

Year 6 female

◼ I use character virtues at home with my brother. When he gives up doing his homework I tell him to use determination.

Year 6 female

◼ I run a lunchtime club and make children feel valued and welcome.

Year 6 male

◼ Character education is something you do 24/7 because it influences everything we do. It's in our blood.

The school works closely with other schools to demonstrate how we can be stronger together. The schools have formed a united front led by Yeading Junior School and linking with WE on campaigns such as the WE 'Walk for Water' and 'WE Are Silent'. We have also invited schools to enjoy and take part in the annual celebration day of social action. One senior leader stated that they 'came away from the event very excited, highly motivated and inspired to put on similar events at our school but you have already set the bar very high!'

Yeading Junior School recognizes the importance of whole families working together on social action. This recognition is also acknowledged in the publication *Transforming Young People and Communities*:

Youth social action has had a huge impact on parental engagement. The passion the students go home with inspires their parents. A father of one of our pupils is now going into work encouraging everyone to think about the difference they can make. (Jubilee Centre 2015, p.6)

The advice in this document is to inspire students with role-models who are strong social action ambassadors and vice versa (e.g. peers, ex-students, parents and grandparents).

Working on campaigns with others

The WE programme encourages children and young people to be instrumental in making changes for communities. The WE 'Walk for Water' enables children to raise funds and awareness of the need for clean water in developing countries; the 'WE Are Silent' campaign encourages the children to again raise awareness and funds for those whose voices are not heard. Yeading Junior School put a plan of action in place and worked with five other schools to raise awareness.

As a result of the strong networks and partnerships (see Chapter 4), we were able to use our local university as a venue for this event and could rely on the training information shared by the WE organization to enable teachers within the schools involved to run a station in the accompanying workshop. Each school was then empowered to take the campaign forward in their own way with their communities. The outcome from the event was that we had empowered 90 children from Year 2 to Year 7 to gain knowledge, work together, think innovatively, learn to undertake social action and measure impact. Each school also raised funds for these events in whatever way possible, inspired by the children. We were delighted that our school raised considerable funds for both events.

The development of character has led to significant changes in how children, staff and families see their role as 'Agents of Change' for others and their real desire to focus on the impact of this change. It is with a sense of pride that individuals and groups are spurred on to encourage others to become successful. A very clear example of this is shown where an older sibling, a 'Special Agent of Change', has been encouraged to work with a younger sibling who presented with some negative behaviour. It was thought that the power of peer mentoring in the mantle of the character virtues would have a positive impact on this younger child and would be beneficial to her welfare. It was proposed to both siblings that we would work together to gain a deeper understanding of the virtues. Furthermore, the younger sibling would be encouraged to engage with the children's Agent leadership team on particular projects. The prospect of working with this group of Agents, as well as being included in specific projects, enabled the younger child to feel that she would have the confidence to transform her behaviour. After two days of striving really hard, the younger sibling displayed improved behaviour and learning. This child also took an active role in the joint schools' campaign around 'WE Are Silent'. Having been especially selected to take part in this, she was delighted by her own success. What is more, the other Special Agents rallied in support of the older sibling.

This was quite conclusive in terms of the children's general deep understanding of the virtues and how by using these we not only impact on ourselves but also others. There is a great understanding amongst the children that people grow and change through our own role modelling. Innovative projects and different learning platforms provide children with opportunities to seek solutions to social issues locally, globally and amongst their peers. This provides a life-long learning opportunity for children and their families.

The phrase 'I just want to be a good human being' was quoted by one of our parents a number of years ago when we set up a community resource for parents and carers. It is this phrase that has helped shape some of the work with our children and staff. Character development has had a significant impact not only on children but also in terms of staff CPD. The initial work within school began with 'Champions' (those members of staff who have embraced character and virtue education and led others to emulate by example), and Champions continue their journey in line with the 'Road to Success' (emblazoned on classroom doors), taking the same turns en route but remaining on a continuum. Finding a committed Champion who is respected by others and clearly demonstrating impact with the children is an imperative for starting the journey. That Champion clearly works with peers and non-teaching staff. The inspired children engage not only their peers but captivate the others across the school through their actions, and their families become so motivated they speak with others in the community. A sea of change occurs, and the language permeates the school. In speaking about the village of education, Ellen Doherty notes:

> Teachers are Agents of Change in their community by working with parents and families to make sure that children are healthy and strong and they are part of that. They transform lives in terms of educational experience, they transform lives in terms of including them in education and society, they transform and change lives in terms of what their life

chances are going to be like. It really does take a village to bring up a child and actually, it is the village of Education. (Doherty 2017)

A child Agent at Yeading Junior School once remarked:

> When you drop a stone in the water it has a ripple effect, just like Character Education – we pass it on.

The success of our character education is that it is shared and ever-growing, embedded in our ethos and known to all. Our Agents are excellent role models, and others are constantly influenced and desirous of following in their footsteps.

References

Cabinet Office (2015) *Social Action: Harnessing the Potential*. Discussion paper. Accessed 19/05/2019 at www.gov.uk/government/publications/social-action-harnessing-the-potential-update

Cleverdon, J. (2018) Personal communication to the children at Yeading Junior School, 30 October 2018.

Department for Education (DfE) (2014) *Listening to and Involving Children and Young People*. Reference: DFE 00011-2014. London: DfE.

Doherty, E. (2017) *Education Talks: Teachers transforming lives*. Accessed 23/09/19 at www.schooleducationgateway.eu/en/pub/viewpoints/interviews/education-talks-teachers-tran.htm

#iwill (n.d.) 'About'. Accessed 08/10/19 at www.iwill.org.uk/about-us/about-iwill-campaign

Jubilee Centre (2015) *Transforming Young People and Communities (#iwill)*. Birmingham: The Jubilee Centre for Character and Virtues (University of Birmingham).

Jubilee Centre (2017) *Framework for Character Education in Schools*. The Jubilee Centre for Character and Virtues (University of Birmingham).

Price-Mitchell, M. (2015) 'Grow a child's empathy in 3 easy ways: Why learning to give back matters'. *Psychology Today*, 11 June. Accessed 20/05/19 at www.psychologytoday.com/gb/blog/the-moment-youth/201506/grow-childs-empathy-in-3-easy-ways

Step Up to Serve (n.d.) *#iwill. About Us*. Accessed 23/08/19 at www.stepuptoserve.org.uk/about-us)

WE Schools (2015–2016) *WE SchoolsGlobal Workbook*.

WE Schools (n.d.) Accessed 25/04/19 at www.we.org

Young Foundation (2013) *Scoping a Quality Framework for Youth Social Action: The Campaign for Youth Social Action*. Accessed 09/05/19 at https://youngfoundation.org/wp-content/uploads/2013/08/Scoping-a-Quality-Framework-for-Youth-Social-Action-FINAL.pdf

Endnote: Where Next for the 'Cultivation of Virtuous Children'?

DAVID ALDRIDGE

How might schools learn from one another?

I have been asked by my colleague Dr Paula Nadine Zwozdiak-Myers to offer some closing thoughts on these inspiring chapters, particularly with a brief to consider next steps and future directions.

One might ask: 'Next steps for whom, and future directions towards what end?' I consider this not to be a work of disinterested 'research' (and would, in any case, want to resist the tyrannical assertion that teachers have only to learn from one or other specifically designated form of research, or stand to be informed only by a narrowly defined type of 'evidence'). Perhaps taken together the chapters constitute a 'case study'; but, more importantly, they are an enticement to thoughtful conversation with a school teaching body, or a group of professionals who have identified some specific practices that constitute a linked endeavour of which they are justly proud, and which they wish to disseminate in order to inspire and learn from others.

Next steps and future directions, then, would be: next steps for the continuation of this conversation; and future directions in which its subject matter might lead us. I'm going to begin – perhaps some might think oddly – by resisting defining too conveniently what the conversation is about. For sure, there is some central vocabulary that might help us to make a hasty sketch map of the general territory in which we are moving. There is a concern with the formation of *character*, the teaching of *values* or *virtues* (if these terms are at all useful, they really ought not to be used interchangeably), and a reflective focus on the *ethos* of the school. In one sense, these are perennial educational themes: what kind of teacher, when pushed, would claim to have no concern or responsibility for the formation of a student's character? Yet these are also concerns which can be connected to a particular set of contemporary foci or influences – a high-profile 'return' to the education of character (largely imported from the USA in recent years as a response to an alleged 'failure' of contemporary approaches to moral education and to problems with maintaining 'discipline' in schools), some large and highly influential projects and university centres for the education of character and value (funded for the most part by a linked set of wealthy and private research foundations), and (in England and Wales at least) the Department for Education initiatives, driven largely by Conservative politicians and connected with other contemporary policy concerns such as the explicit teaching of fundamental 'British' values and the prevention of terrorism.

These two strands – the perennial educational concerns and the more contemporary (one could rightly say 'political') ones – might not be closely connected; we might have to trace the conversational threads quite a way back before we find their common roots. So, I would urge that we ought to beware of false friends in our terminology. Just because we are likely concerned with the formation of our students' character does not mean that we necessarily support 'character education' in any formal or explicit sense. The formation of character is going to mean very different things for different educators. This might seem like a truism, but it is worth emphasizing that in terms of education's normative aims we are not dealing with settled matters. We do not 'know', once and for all, what ethical aims education is trying to achieve – or at least, we should not be so certain of our desired ends that we hold them to be unquestionable. This recognition gives some shape and at the same time sets some limits to the ways in which we might hope to learn from each other in our conversation around (broadly) the formation of character and the cultivation of virtue in schools.

The primary value of this conversation can hardly be that lessons might be generalized, transferred or applied from one context to another. One school's ethos differs from another's – in many cases quite considerably. But it is precisely because our partners in dialogue differ from us that we stand to learn from them. Educators coming into the conversation about character formation have already taken a standpoint on matters that are rightly contested, or at least are contestable. The value of the conversation is that it will bring our settled assumptions into question and open up new imaginative possibilities for future practice. In the spirit of this kind of dialogue, I offer as my contribution the posing of a couple of questions for further consideration (implying some of my own, initial and admittedly partial, answers), as well as presenting a provocative quotation.

How Aristotelian does my character education need to be?

In explicitly invoking the language of character and virtue, as well as by referring to the work of the University of Birmingham's Jubilee Centre for Character and Virtue, the authors of many of these chapters are aligning their standpoint with a resurgence of emphasis on broadly Aristotelian ideas about moral formation and education more generally. One insight commonly attributed to Aristotle is the recognition that being good involves more than simply knowing what is right and wrong. One needs only to point to any number of highly intelligent people (I am thinking of one or two public figures as I write this!) who cannot reasonably be considered to be deficient in moral knowledge, but who nevertheless do not do the right thing. This has been referred to as the 'gappiness problem', referring to the gap that is sometimes found between moral belief and moral behaviour. The implication is that educators concerned with moral formation should be paying attention to the ways that this gap can be bridged. Aristotelian moral educators claim that a focus on the 'cognitive' aspect of moral education – whether this means directively offering moral guidance or engaging in reflective dialogue to clarify a student's individual moral standpoint – is insufficient, since important moral habits are formed before children are susceptible to such instruction.

Hence the focus on 'character'. We say that a person is of good character when they not only know or say the right thing, but also do it consistently and reliably, even when it causes them inconvenience or discomfort. The education of character, the Aristotelian moral educator argues, requires paying attention not only to moral knowledge but also to the development of a collection of relatively stable traits (the 'virtues'); it is because he or she is in possession of the virtues that an individual can be said to be good (or morally flourishing), not because he or she is in possession of a particular bit of moral knowledge or even because he or she has acted in a particular way at a particular time. Moral education, therefore, has not only cognitive components (although the ability to know or discern the right thing to do is important) but also affective (*feeling* appropriately disgusted or impressed by morally repugnant or praiseworthy acts), conative (*wanting* to do the right thing as well as knowing what it is) and behavioural (having the resilience or other capacity to go through with it). The virtues take in elements of perception (they involve developing the capacity to see particular actions or entities in a particular way) as well as disposition (inclination and ability to act on what has been perceived as such).

Some might argue that intervention in the development of such dispositions is largely beyond the responsibility of most school teachers, who might reasonably be expected to deal only with moral knowledge (if they have a responsibility for moral development *at all*). The Aristotelian moral educator, however, replies that whether a teacher likes it or not, he or she is deeply implicated in such processes. The formation of moral virtues, it is argued, particularly in the early years, is not largely due to explicit cognitive interventions, but rather to a process of habituation. Before they can offer or understand reasons for behaving one way rather than another, children emulate the models or examples that are presented to them, and associate pleasure and displeasure in accordance with rewards and sanctions that are applied to them (including praise or censure). Teachers, second only to parents and in some cases even more so, constitute a consistent adult presence in the lives of young children, offering examples (consciously or otherwise) of moral conduct, and liberally indulging in systems of morally significant reward and sanction. We might add that the Aristotelian educator observes no clear distinction between moral development and other kinds of schoolwork, since academic success requires the development of intellectual virtues.

Much of this is well taken, but it is worth acknowledging that a 'turn' to character education is often accompanied by a deficit model of morality. The Aristotelian approach to moral education is often presented as a return to some common-sense educational activity that has been harmed in recent years by a supposed relativist squeamishness. Teachers, it is argued, need not only to get over their concerns about telling students what it is right and wrong to do, or (as they get older) engaging them in reasoned discussion about morality, but also need to be self-consciously modelling virtuous behaviour for their students, explicitly rewarding and praising it, consistently sanctioning wrongdoing and exhibiting disgust at immoral activity.

I am not so convinced that moral education has 'gone wrong', as is sometimes suggested, over 50–60 years of *laissez-faire* progressive education. This often seems to me to be the convenient construction of a problem to which character education can be presented as a solution. Rather than as a solution, I tend to see Aristotelian character education as presenting a particular set of questions to educators. These include the question of how exemplarity or modelling works, what kind of pedagogy there can be for habituation, and how confident we can be as educators of the state of our knowledge of the appropriate virtues to be delivered.

With regard to the first of these questions, it should be observed that children cannot at any stage emulate exemplars without interpreting them. Consider the child who emulates a parent by castigating or instructing a younger sibling. The parent might intervene, explaining that it is their own responsibility to castigate or instruct, not the child's. This intervention is the parent's attempt to specify the ways in which he or she intends to be taken as an exemplar, and the ways in which he or she does not. There is very little, in fact, in the parent's interaction with a child which can simply be 'read off' as an example of an action to be imitated. Rather, the child must come to understand the spirit of what is offered. This is no less the case with teachers, who in their institutional roles perform all sorts of actions which children are not directly intended to imitate. Children are expected to emulate the virtues being modelled rather than the actions that result from the particular ways that these virtues are instantiated in the role of a teacher. But to infer the virtues from their contextual instantiations requires a considerable amount of interpretive work on the part of the child. This could be addressed consciously with the age-old method of instructing children in the ways that one intends to be taken as an exemplar – 'imitate this action of mine, not that one' – but such an intervention does not stand outside of the circle of interpretation. Rather, it performs another kind of intellectual model that the learning child is expected to understand and emulate.

This suggests that there is an unacknowledged 'gappiness problem' in character education – the 'gap' between the intended educational function of exemplarity and its reception by the student. This is a gap that is bridged by dialogue, so that character education cannot involve simply showing or telling children what to do, even at the level of habituation. Dialogue here does not mean simply talking with children, since this process of moral habituation begins before they can engage in spoken conversation. To say that character education is dialogic means that *right from the start* it involves engaging children's developing interpretive capacities.

This dialogic insight problematizes simpler ideas we might have about an appropriate pedagogy for character education. Consider the case when a particular moral exemplar is offered to students – a visiting speaker, say, or a great work of literary or cinematic art – and the majority of students are moved to tears or another strong emotional response. This event speaks strongly of the power of the speaker or text, to be sure, but at least as much of the humanity or sensitivity of the audience who were able to receive and respond to the exemplar in this way. If we extend this dialogic insight into our own recognition and awareness, as educators, of the moral virtues, we accept that this too involves a rich interpretive component, which ought to introduce some caution into our claims to know with considerable certainty the particular virtues that need to be communicated to our students.

Have we got the virtues (or values) right?

It is becoming increasingly popular for schools to specify a list of virtues or values which constitute their ethos, and which are addressed explicitly in their pedagogical practice. Such lists are more and more commonly inscribed into the very architecture of our schools and undergo something like a memetic transfer from one school reception wall to another. Of course, there is something arbitrary about any such list that a teaching body might decide to 'double down' on in this way. It also goes without saying that any school ethos we might be inclined to value will resist expression in such a necessarily reductive list. (It is satisfying to note, incidentally, that ethos, which also gives rise to our word 'ethics', is the word used by the ancient Greek writers to denote what we often translate as 'character'). School ethos, we have noted above, differs from school to school, but what also differs are the perceptions different parents, teachers and students have of the *same* school. While members of the school community and interested stakeholders might agree that there is something of value in the ethos and atmosphere of a school, this is often something that is difficult to express, or to agree on expressing, in anything but the most simplistic terms (notwithstanding the fact that all schools in England and Wales are required to post explicit public statements of their aims, purpose and ethos on their websites, so that a very banal sort of language has emerged in which to make such attempts).

Rather than proving comprehensive, such lists of values or virtues will exhibit ambiguities and even tensions on extended investigation. Such tensions are in evidence in the collection of chapters presented here by members of the same teaching body. One example is the tension between the presentation of financial education and the innovative use of 'Yeadoes' to incentivize students to behave appropriately, with the recognition elsewhere of the need for students to be intrinsically rather than extrinsically motivated. There is no doubt that financial prudence is a vital element of flourishing existence in our contemporary situation, and that the use of Yeadoes has been recognized and praised by experts as both an innovative and successful way of encouraging economic literacy. Yet there is also the possibility that such strategies might privilege a consideration of certain desirable aspects of behaviour, intellectual engagement and human relations as leading to economic benefits, when it might be hoped that for a flourishing life such moral goods come to be seen as desirable in themselves.

Now, one might be inclined to think of such tensions as mixed or conflicting messages, but this is only the case if we are inclined to think of the cultivation of virtue in terms of the giving of messages. It seems to me that something much less direct is implied. A useful analogy might be found in the way that literature or art functions as a morally educative medium. The development of moral sensibility is closely related to the development of aesthetic sensibility, in that we come to be more sensitive, through exposure, to the salient aspects of moral situations in a similar way to that in which we become more discerning of literary expression and significance through increasing exposure to texts. The two are also intertwined, in that we can become more sensitive to moral significance through exposure to morally charged texts. But some violence is done to this process, or some link in the chain is broken, at the point when an educator presents a particular passage with the intention of its 'teaching' a particular virtue. It is in the nature of any works of art or literature worthy of the name (even those intended for very young readers) that they are subject to a richness and variety of interpretations, and it is in the nature of young people's imaginative dialogic interactions with texts that they will come to understandings that will surprise teachers and subvert or frustrate any intended moral message. 'Correction' is hardly the appropriate pedagogical strategy to employ in such a situation. It is in the nature of any moral development that comes through aesthetic engagement with art and literature that it is a gradual, emergent process that is not greatly assisted by explicit efforts to guide students towards a particular interpretation with directive moral intent.

So it might be, I imagine, with a child's engagement with the ethos of a school. There are not simple meanings to be read off from the school community or a teacher's particular pedagogical decisions, any more than there are clear moral messages to be read off literary texts or artworks. It may be that it is the desire for clarity that is out of place where the cultivation of virtue is concerned. The ambiguity that characterizes a school's ethos, core values, and even its educational aims is a strength in the sense that it reflects the kind of ambiguity that emerges in human community and results from the fact that schools form parts of a diverse society in which moral matters are far from cut and dried.

It seems to me that schools should maybe not be too concerned about whether they have got their list of virtues or values 'right' – since they can hardly hope to have done so. But they should perhaps also be wary of taking up a chisel to etch them into the wall. What matters is not that schools have their values 'right', but that they take seriously that something is valued by a community (members of that community might not agree on exactly what), that something of great importance for a flourishing life and a healthy world is at stake here, and that there is therefore a responsibility to engage students in this question of what is to be valued. But it is also vital that if this offer is to be educative, it must be presented as questionable, revisable, and emergent in dialogue with students and wider society. The point of books such as this is that teachers are hereby having the conversation about what value offer they are making to students.

'We are social engineers'

I heard this claim, which was presented quite uncontroversially, at an international gathering of academics working in moral education that I attend annually. I admit that I found it quite shocking. In particular, it unapologetically connected moral development with a kind of technical rationalism, which in many discussions of a sociological nature is often itself presented as liable to erode moral meaning. Moral development, it implied, in the manner of other technologies or forms of engineering, can be increasingly perfected through engagement with scientific research so that it brings about its intended result ever more efficiently.

The lure of seeing moral formation as a technological endeavour is that it is subject to the eventual refinement of its proper pedagogical methods for the minimization of loss of time and resources and the misdirection of energy; hence, the regular emphasis in discussions of school ethos and moral leadership on clarity, explicitness and confident vision. What I hope to have introduced into the ongoing conversation is a sense of the kind of subtlety and tact (or 'feeling around') that might be required if we accept that our educational aims are emergent, or that we don't quite know (we can't yet 'put our finger on') what we are trying to achieve.

In such a situation it is also not clear that we will be able to find ways of measuring the impact of our interventions into virtue. It is written into Aristotelian virtue ethics that it is consistency over the long haul, rather than a snapshot view of a particular action or expressed belief that will disclose the nature of a life lived virtuously. Teachers know that it is often very many years later, if at all, that we will see the fruits of our endeavours as regards the good character of our students.

One child at Yeading Junior School, cited by the headteacher in Chapter 1, highlights the importance of believing that 'you were born to change the world'. This is a belief that it is vital not only to impress on students but also to remember as teachers. What does moral education look like if educators keep in mind that children are born to change the world, or even to save it from our own poor efforts? While it does not mean abandoning our moral offer (at the same time thereby abandoning children to come up with something by themselves), it does mean entertaining the possibility that we do not know enough about our children's future to assume that the moral imagination that has served us will serve them equally well. It is fitting, I hope, to close with that insight from one of the pupils at Yeading Junior School, as I also want to suggest that dialogue, attentive listening to children, and responsiveness to students' push-back or openness to our attempts at moral guidance, are essential components of any educational endeavours to cultivate virtue.

Appendix A: Key Principles for/of Character Education

	Key Principles for Character Education (Jubilee Centre 2017)	The 11 Principles of Effective Character (Character.org n.d.)
1	Character is educable and its progress can be assessed holistically.	The school community promotes core ethical and performance values as the foundation of good character.
2	Character is important: it contributes to human and societal flourishing.	The school defines 'character' comprehensively to include thinking, feeling and doing.
3	Good education is good character education.	The school uses a comprehensive, intentional, and proactive approach to character development.
4	Character is largely caught through role-modelling and emotional contagion; school culture and ethos are therefore central.	The school creates a caring community.
5	A school culture that enables students to satisfy their needs for positive relationships, competence and self-determination facilitates the acquisition of good character.	The school provides students with opportunities for moral action.
6	Character should also be taught; direct teaching of character provides the rationale, language and tools to use in developing character elsewhere in and out of school.	The school offers a meaningful and challenging academic curriculum that respects all learners, develops their character and helps them to succeed.
7	Character should be developed in partnership with parents, employers and other community organizations.	The school fosters students' self-motivation.

cont.

	Key Principles for Character Education (Jubilee Centre 2017)	The 11 Principles of Effective Character (Character.org n.d.)
8	Character education is about fairness, and each child has a right to character development.	The school staff is an ethical learning community that shares responsibility for character education and adheres to the same core values that guide the students.
9	Positive character development empowers students and is liberating.	The school fosters shared leadership and long-range support of the character education initiative.
10	Good character demonstrates a readiness to learn from others.	The school engages families and community members as partners in the character-building effort.
11	Good character promotes democratic citizenship and autonomous decision-making.	The school regularly assesses its culture and climate, the functioning of its staff as character educators, and the extent to which its students manifest good character.

Source: Jubilee Centre (2017) *A Framework for Character Education in Schools.* Birmingham: The Jubilee Centre for Character and Virtues (University of Birmingham). Accessed 08/27/18 at www.jubileecentre.ac.uk

Character.org (n.d.) *The 11 Principles of Effective Character.* Accessed 10/04/19 at www.character.org/character

Appendix B: Promoting Fundamental British Values as Part of SMSC in Schools

Schools should promote the fundamental British values of democracy, the rule of law, individual liberty, and mutual respect and tolerance of those with different faiths and beliefs... Through their provision of Social, Moral, Spiritual and Cultural (SMSC) education, schools should:

- enable students to develop their self-knowledge, self-esteem and self-confidence;
- enable students to distinguish right from wrong and to respect the civil and criminal law of England;
- encourage students to accept responsibility for their behaviour, show initiative, and to understand how they can contribute positively to the lives of those living and working in the locality of the school and to society more widely;
- enable students to acquire a broad general knowledge of and respect for public institutions and services in England;
- further tolerance and harmony between different cultural traditions by enabling students to acquire an appreciation of and respect for their own and other cultures;
- encourage respect for other people; and
- encourage respect for democracy and support participation in the democratic processes, including respect for the basis on which the law is made and applied in England.

The list below describes the understanding and knowledge expected of pupils as a result of schools promoting fundamental British values:

- an understanding of how citizens can influence decision-making through the democratic process;
- an appreciation that living under the rule of law protects individual citizens and is essential for their wellbeing and safety;

- an understanding that there is a separation of power between the executive and the judiciary, and that while some public bodies such as the police and the army can be held to account through Parliament, others such as the courts maintain independence;
- an understanding that the freedom to choose and hold other faiths and beliefs is protected in law;
- an acceptance that other people having different faiths or beliefs to oneself (or having none) should be accepted and tolerated, and should not be the cause of prejudicial or discriminatory behaviour; and
- an understanding of the importance of identifying and combatting discrimination.

It is not necessary for schools or individuals to 'promote' teachings, beliefs or opinions that conflict with their own, but nor is it acceptable for schools to promote discrimination against people or groups on the basis of their belief, opinion or background.

(Department for Education [DfE] [2014] *Promoting fundamental British values as part of SMSC. Departmental advice for maintained schools.* Accessed 24/9/19 at https://assets.publishing.service.gov.uk/government/uploads/system/uploads/attachment_data/file/380595/SMSC_Guidance_Maintained_Schools.pdf)

Appendix C: Classification of 6 Virtues and 24 Character Strengths

1. Wisdom and knowledge – cognitive strengths that entail the acquisition and use of knowledge

Creativity [originality, ingenuity]: Thinking of novel and productive ways to conceptualize and do things; includes artistic achievement but is not limited to it

Curiosity [interest, novelty-seeking, openness to experience]: Taking an interest in ongoing experience for its own sake; finding subjects and topics fascinating; exploring and discovering

Open-mindedness [judgment, critical thinking]: Thinking things through and examining them from all sides; not jumping to conclusions; being able to changes one's mind in light of evidence; weighing all evidence fairly

Love of learning: Mastering new skills, topics, and bodies of knowledge, whether on one's own or formally; obviously related to the strength of curiosity but goes beyond it to describe the tendency to add systematically to what one knows

Perspective [wisdom]: Being able to provide wise counsel to others; having ways of looking at the world that make sense to oneself and to other people

2. Courage – emotional strengths that involve the exercise of will to accomplish goals in the face of opposition, external or internal

Bravery [valor]: Not shrinking from threat, challenge, difficulty, or pain; speaking up for what is right even if there is opposition; acting on convictions even if unpopular; includes physical bravery but is not limited to it

Persistence [perseverance, industriousness]: Finishing what one starts; persisting in a course of action in spite of obstacles; "getting it out the door"; taking pleasure in completing tasks

Integrity [authenticity, honesty]: Speaking the truth but more broadly presenting oneself in a genuine way and acting in a sincere way; being without pretense; taking responsibility for one's feelings and actions

Vitality [zest, enthusiasm, vigor, energy]: Approaching life with excitement and energy; not doing things halfway or halfheartedly; living life as an adventure; feeling alive and activated

3. Humanity – interpersonal strengths that involve tending and befriending others

Love: Valuing close relations with others, in particular those in which sharing and caring are reciprocated; being close to people

Kindness [generosity, nurturance, care, compassion, altruistic love, "niceness"]: Doing favors and good deeds for others; helping them; taking care of them

Social intelligence [emotional intelligence, personal intelligence]: Being aware of the motives and feelings of other people and oneself; knowing what to do to fit into different social situations; knowing what makes other people tick

4. Justice – civic strengths that underlie healthy community life

Citizenship [social responsibility, loyalty, teamwork]: Working well as a member of a group or team; being loyal to the group; doing one's share

Fairness: Treating all people the same according to notions of fairness and justice; not letting personal feelings bias decisions about others; giving everyone a fair chance

Leadership: Encouraging a group of which one is a member to get things done and at the same time maintain good relations within the group; organizing group activities and seeing that they happen

5. Temperance – strengths that protect against excess

Forgiveness and mercy: Forgiving those who have done wrong; accepting the shortcomings of others; giving people a second chance; not being vengeful

Humility/Modesty: Letting one's accomplishments speak for themselves; not seeking the spotlight; not regarding oneself as more special than one is

Prudence: Being careful about one's choices; not taking undue risks; not saying or doing things that might later be regretted

Self-regulation [self-control]: Regulating what one feels and does; being disciplined; controlling one's appetites and emotions

6. Transcendence – strengths that forge connections to the larger universe and provide meaning

Appreciation of beauty and excellence [awe, wonder, elevation]: Noticing and appreciating beauty, excellence, and/or skilled performance in various domains of life, from nature to art to mathematics to science to everyday experience

Gratitude: Being aware of and thankful for the good things that happen; taking time to express thanks

Hope [optimism, future-mindedness, future orientation]: Expecting the best in the future and working to achieve it; believing that a good future is something that can be brought about

Humor [playfulness]: Liking to laugh and tease; bringing smiles to other people; seeing the light side; making (not necessarily telling) jokes

Spirituality [religiousness, faith, purpose]: Having coherent beliefs about the higher purpose and meaning of the universe; knowing where one fits within the larger scheme; having beliefs about the meaning of life that shape conduct and provide comfort

Source © Peterson, C. and Seligman, M. (2004) *Character Strengths and Virtues: A Handbook and Classification.* Washington, DC: American Psychological Association, pp.29–30.

Reproduced with permission of the Licensor through PLSclear.

Contributors' Biographies

David Aldridge is Director of Research in the Department of Education at Brunel University London. His research interests include philosophy of education, moral education, and the relation of technology, science and education. He is particularly interested in the ways that educational thought can draw on the resources of literary theory and expression.

Jean-Michel Ballay is Assistant Headteacher at Yeading Junior School and a specialist teacher of Modern Foreign Languages (French and Spanish). He has a particularly keen interest in language acquisition and the teaching of Classics.

Angela Flux taught in three secondary schools and then served most of her adult life as Head of Health Promotion/Public Health with Local Government and NHS Hillingdon, specializing in wellbeing programmes, managing drugs prevention, and sexual health and counselling services for adolescents. Working with the Institute of Education and University College London, she has pioneered and researched peer education and support within educational settings. She is currently Chair of Governors in two schools (Yeading Junior School and Hillside Infants), manages the MHA Northwood Live at Home Scheme and is developing a community-based approach to multi-generational programmes and partnerships.

Carole Jones, Headteacher at Yeading Junior School, is passionate about working with the wider community and partners to develop children's social action. She has introduced character education into the school, including a set of virtues which are embedded in the ethos and threaded across the curriculum. She actively promotes volunteering and is a trustee of the Hillingdon Community Trust. In her role as Headteacher, she also chairs a number of committees.

David Moran is a Year 3 teacher and Financial Education Coordinator at Yeading Junior School. Particular educational interests include real-life learning of Financial Education in Mathematics and the importance of Physical Education for children.

Elenor Paul has been RE Coordinator at Yeading Junior School since 2010 and is the advisor to Hillingdon Standing Advisory Council on Religious Education (SACRE). She is also a visiting lecturer at Brunel University London where she teaches on the PGCE (Post Graduate Certificate in Education) programme. Particular research interests include the provision of Religious Education within the primary school.

Paula Nadine Zwozdiak-Myers is senior lecturer and Programme Director for the Doctor of Education (EdD) at Brunel University London. She is also course leader for the Master of Arts in Teaching, and specialist pathway lead for the 'Social Justice, Equity and Inclusion' strand of the Master of Arts in Education programme. Particular research interests include reflective practice for professional development in teacher education, pedagogical strategies for inclusive education and cultivating positive habits of mind in children and young people.

Subject Index

Author Index